T0319030

Cambridge Elements

Elements in Perception
edited by
James T. Enns
The University of British Columbia

ATTENDING TO MOVING OBJECTS

Alex Holcombe
The University of Sydney

Shaftesbury Road, Cambridge CB2 8EA, United Kingdom

One Liberty Plaza, 20th Floor, New York, NY 10006, USA

477 Williamstown Road, Port Melbourne, VIC 3207, Australia

314–321, 3rd Floor, Plot 3, Splendor Forum, Jasola District Centre, New Delhi – 110025, India

103 Penang Road, #05–06/07, Visioncrest Commercial, Singapore 238467

Cambridge University Press is part of Cambridge University Press & Assessment, a department of the University of Cambridge.

We share the University's mission to contribute to society through the pursuit of education, learning and research at the highest international levels of excellence.

www.cambridge.org
Information on this title: www.cambridge.org/9781009009973
DOI: 10.1017/9781009003414

First published 2023

A catalogue record for this publication is available from the British Library.

ISBN 978-1-009-00997-3 Paperback
ISSN 2515-0502 (online)
ISSN 2515-0499 (print)

Additional resources for this publication at www.cambridge.org/Holcombe_supplementary

Attending to Moving Objects

Elements in Perception

DOI: 10.1017/9781009003414
First published online: January 2023

Alex Holcombe
The University of Sydney

Author for correspondence: Alex Holcombe, alex.holcombe@sydney.edu.au

Abstract: Our minds are severely limited in how much information they can extensively process, in spite of being massively parallel at the visual end. When people attempt to track moving objects, only a limited number can be tracked, which varies with display parameters. Associated experiments indicate that spatial selection and updating have higher capacity than selection and updating of features such as color and shape, and are mediated by processes specific to each cerebral hemisphere, such that each hemifield has its own spatial tracking limit. These spatial selection processes act as a bottleneck that gates subsequent processing. To improve our understanding of this bottleneck, future works should strive to avoid contamination of tracking tasks by high-level cognition. While we are far from fully understanding how attention keeps up with multiple moving objects, what we already know illuminates the architecture of visual processing and offers promising directions for new discoveries.

Keywords: tracking, attention, perception, multiple object tracking, serial processing

ISBNs: 9781009009973 (PB), 9781009003414 (OC)
ISSNs: 2515-0502 (online), 2515-0499 (print)

Contents

1 Objects That Move

Attention is "the taking possession by the mind, in clear and vivid form, of one out of what seem several simultaneously possible objects or trains of thought." At least that is how William James described it (James, 1890). James' description seems to imply that attention has a limited capacity of just one object or train of thought. James was joined at Harvard in 1892 by Hugo Münsterberg, who used moving stimuli to study attention. Münsterberg published a book in 1916, *The Photoplay: A Psychological Study*, which described his theory of the "moving pictures" (the cinema) and included a chapter on attention.

Münsterberg's book is insightful, but he did not address how attention operates in the presence of multiple moving stimuli. Much later, after World War II, the study of attention grew rapidly, and tachistoscopes became the

Figure 1 This "complication apparatus" from the Harvard laboratory of Hugo Münsterberg was used to measure the effect of attention to one stimulus on responses to another. A subject who focused on one of the numbers on the large dial was found to have a delayed reaction to the sound of the bell, and vice versa.

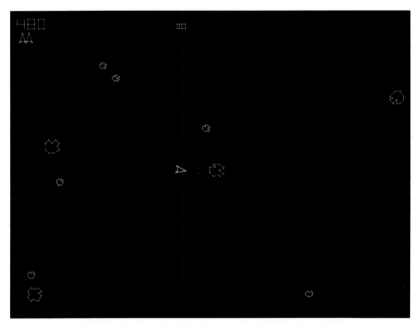

Video 1 Asteroids was released by Atari in 1979. Note: an animated version of the figure is available in the online resources (www.cambridge.org/Holcombe_supplementary)

standard laboratory presentation apparatus. These devices were limited in that they could not present motion: they were designed to present static stimuli very briefly. The dominance of stationary stimuli in the study of attention continued through the 1980s, even as the study of motion grew in a separate community of perception researchers.

The first popular home game system, the Atari, introduced the game Space Invaders in 1980 to millions of homes, including those of some of my childhood friends. Asteroids was ported to the Atari soon after, and it became one of my favorites.

When one plays Space Invaders or Asteroids (Video 1), multiple objects frequently move in the direction of one's avatar. Avoiding a collision seems to require monitoring more than one of these objects at a time. The ability of humans to do this was formally studied first by the Canadian psychologist and engineer Zenon Pylyshyn.

In the 1970s, Zenon Pylyshyn had been pondering the possibility of a primitive visual mechanism capable of "indexing and tracking features or feature-clusters" (he mentions this in Pylyshyn and Storm [1988]; I haven't been able to get copies of the 1970s reports that he refers to) as they moved. By 1988, Zenon Pylyshyn and Ron Storm formulated a way to empirically study

Video 2 A demonstration of the MOT task, created by Jiri Lukavsky.
Note: an animated version of the figure is available in the online resources
(www.cambridge.org/Holcombe_supplementary)

his hypothesized primitive visual mechanism, and they did a series of experiments on humans' ability to keep track of moving objects (Pylyshyn and Storm, 1988). On their Apple II+ computer, they created a display with ten identical objects moving on random trajectories, connected to a telegraph key with a timer to record response times. Pylyshyn and Storm also pioneered the use of an eyetracker to enforce fixation – in their experiments, movement of the eyes away from fixation terminated a trial. Thus they were able to investigate the ability to covertly (without eye movements) keep track of moving objects.

In a task that Pylyshyn and Storm dubbed multiple object tracking (MOT), up to five of ten displayed moving objects were designated as targets by flashing at the beginning of the trial. The targets then became identical to the remaining moving objects, the distractors, and moved about randomly. While viewing the display, people report having the experience of being aware, seemingly continually, of which objects are the targets and how they are moving about. In the movie embedded in Video 2, one is first asked to track a single target to become familiar with the task, and then subsequently four targets are indicated.

In addition to their demonstration that people could do the basic task, which in itself is quite important, Pylyshyn and Storm (1988) also showed that people are limited in *how many* targets they can faithfully track. In their experiments, Pylyshyn and Storm (1988) periodically flashed one of the moving objects, and if that object was a target, the participant was to press the telegraph key.

On trials with more targets, errors were much more common: while only 2% of target flashes were missed when only one of the ten objects was a target, 14% of target flashes were missed when five of the objects were targets.

The notion of keeping track of moving objects is familiar from certain situations in everyday life. If you've ever been responsible for more than one child while at a beach or a park, you know the feeling of continuously monitoring the locations of multiple moving objects. If you've ever played a team sport, you may recall the feeling of monitoring the positions of multiple opponents at the same time, perhaps the player with the ball and also a player they might pass the ball to. If you've ever wanted to speak to someone at a conference, you may know the feeling of monitoring the position and posture of that person relative to others they are chatting with, in order to best time your approach.

1.1 What's to Come

Despite advances in technology, the study of visual cognition continues to be dominated by experiments with stimuli that don't move. As we'll see in Section 10, putting objects in motion reveals that updating of their representations is not as effective as one might expect from studies with static stimuli. This suggests that with static objects, one can bring to bear additional processes, perhaps cognitive processes (Section 6), that motion helps to dissociate from lower-level tracking processes. It is these sorts of unique insights from MOT experiments that I have chosen to emphasize in this Element, together with the findings that I believe most constrain theories of how mental tracking processes work. I will argue that the following are the five most important findings in the MOT literature:

1. The number of moving objects humans can track is limited, but not to a particular number such as four or five (Section 3).
2. The number of targets has little effect on spatial interference, whereas it greatly increases temporal interference (Section 5).
3. Predictability of movement paths benefits tracking only for one or two targets, not for more (Section 6).
4. Tracking capacity is hemifield-specific: capacity nearly doubles when targets are presented in different hemifields (Section 9).
5. When tracking multiple targets, people often don't know which target is which, and updating of nonlocation features is poor (Section 10).

The organization of this Element was influenced by my desire to dispel common misconceptions about results in the literature, and to lay out the concepts needed to understand the implications of the empirical findings. In Section 13

I describe some broad lessons, including how best to study tracking in the future. We will start with the concept of limited capacity and bottlenecks in the brain.

2 Bottlenecks, Resources, and Capacity

Quickly, what is fourteen times thirteen? Calculating that in your head takes a while, at least a few seconds. And if I set you two such problems rather than just one, I'm confident that you would do those problems one at a time. Our minds seem to be completely incapable of doing two such problems simultaneously (Oberauer, 2002; Zylberberg et al., 2010). This limitation is remarkable given that each of our brains contains more than eighty billion neurons. The problem is not a lack of neurons, really, but how they are arranged – our mental architecture.

Multiplying and dividing two-digit numbers may not be something you attempt to do every day. You might think, then, that if you were doing lots of such problems each day, you could eventually do more than one at a time. This is probably wrong – consider that a task we do have daily practice with is reading. Despite years of reading dozens if not hundreds of words a day, the evidence suggests that humans can read at most only a few words at a time, and some research further indicates that we can really only read *one* word at a time (Reichle et al., 2009; White et al., 2018). At least some of the bottlenecks of human information processing, then, appear to be a fixed property of our processing architecture.

To flesh out what I mean by "bottleneck" here, consider a standard soft drink bottle. If you invert a full bottle, most of the liquid volume will be pressing down on the neck. The narrowness of the neck restricts the rate at which the liquid can exit the bottle. Similarly, a large volume of signals from sensory cortex ascending the cortical hierarchy press up against higher areas that are more limited in capacity.

The parallel processing happening in visual cortices, such as the multiple neurons dedicated to each patch of the visual field, gets a number of tasks done, so that higher stages don't have to do those tasks. These tasks appear to include the encoding of motion direction, color, and orientation throughout the visual field. Local and regional differencing operations happen for those features, resulting in salience, whereby odd features become conspicuous in our visual awareness. In Figure 2, for example, you should be able to find the blue objects very quickly.

For other judgments, higher, post-bottleneck brain areas that are very limited in capacity are critical. The visual word form area in the occipitotemporal sulcus of the left hemisphere, which seems to be needed to recognize words, is

Perception

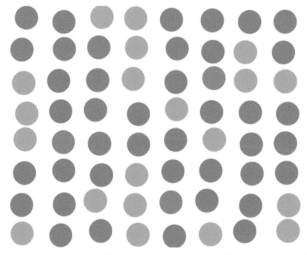

Figure 2 Thanks to featural attention (to color in this case), you should be able to find the blue circles very quickly

one example (White et al., 2019). Being limited in processing capacity to just one stimulus, the word recognition will not happen in a crowded scene until something selectively directs the visual signals from a word to the visual word form area. We often use the term *selective attention* to refer to this "something" that directs particular visual signals to the bottlenecks of limited-capacity processes. If there were no bottlenecks, there would be no need for selection for cognition (selection would be required when an action needed to be chosen).

So far the picture I have painted has been one of a torrent of visual signals impinging on a narrow bottleneck of signals that continue onward. But cortical processing is rarely a one-way street, and the way visual attention works is no exception. Visual attention seems to work partly by biasing processing within visual cortices, rather than leaving that unchanged and blocking all but a few signals at a later bottleneck stage. Thus, processing capacity may be restricted by limitations on control signals from high-level (possibly parietal) cortex that restrict processing capacity, as well as the more familiar idea of a structural bottleneck where ascending visual signals reach a lower-capacity neural mechanism.

To the extent control signals are a limitation, a resource metaphor can be apt. The control of selection may reflect a finite pool of neural resources in parietal cortex that bias which visual signals are cognitively processed. Thus I will sometimes use the term "limited resource" when referring to how we are restricted in how many visual representations are processed.

The word "resource" carries the appropriate connotation that people can choose how to apply their finite processing capacity; ordinarily a resource is something that can be used in different ways. For example, the term suggests that one might use three-quarters of one's processing capacity for one target while using the other quarter for a second target. And indeed, there is evidence that people can favor one target over another when tracking both (Chen et al., 2013; Crowe et al., 2019).

While word recognition seems to be able to process only one stimulus at a time, other visual judgments may be limited in capacity relative to massively parallel sensory processing, but have a capacity greater than one. Object tracking seems to be one such ability. People appear able to track more than one target at the same time, although researchers haven't fully ruled out the possibility that tracking multiple objects happens via a one-by-one process that rapidly switches among the tracked objects.

The existence of processes with a capacity of just one object (I will introduce the term "System B" for this in Section 6) is a good reason to have a process that can keep track of the location of important objects in a scene. We are then always ready to rapidly shunt a subset of them to higher-level processing, rather than having to search for it.

3 The Biggest Myth of Object Tracking

What I consider to be the biggest myth about object tracking involves three misconceptions:

1. There is a fixed capacity limit of about four or five objects that can be tracked, after which performance falls rapidly.
2. A softer version of the above claim: that performance falls to a particular level once the number of targets is increased to four or five objects.
3. Different tasks show the same limit.

These three claims are widespread in the scholarly literature. A set of researchers writing about the "object tracking system" in 2010, for example, stated: "One of the defining properties of this system is that it is limited in capacity to three to four individuals at a time" (Piazza, 2010). Similarly, Fougnie and Marois (2006) wrote that "People's ability to attentively track a number of randomly moving objects among like distractors is limited to four or five items." This idea is sometimes perpetuated with more ambiguous statements such as "participants can track about four objects simultaneously" (Van der Burg et al., 2019).

Misconception #1 in my list, including the idea of a sharp fall in performance after a limit, is one aspect of the statements of the previous paragraph. This is fully explicit in one set of researchers' 2010 take on the literature, when they wrote that "the main finding" of the object tracking literature is that "observers can accurately track approximately four objects and that once this limit is exceeded, accuracy declines precipitously" (Doran and Hoffman, 2010). Vaguer statements in other papers, such as "researchers have consistently found that approximately 4 objects can be tracked" (Alvarez and Franconeri, 2007) and "people typically can track four or five items" Chesney and Haladjian (2011), also bolster misconception #1 in the minds of readers.

To examine the evidence behind the claims of each of the quotations of the two preceding paragraphs, I have checked the evidence provided, and the papers cited, as well as the papers those cited papers cite. No paper contains any evidence supporting the claim that performance decreases very rapidly once the number of targets is increased above some value. Instead, a gradual decrease in performance is seen as the number of targets is increased, with no discontinuity, not even a conspicuous inflection point. For example, Oksama and Hyönä (2004), which is sometimes cited in this context, assessed performance with up to six targets. After a five-second phase of random motion of the multiple moving objects, one object was flashed repeatedly and participants hit a key to indicate whether they thought it was one of the targets. The number of trials that participants got wrong increased steadily with target number, from 3% incorrect with two targets to 16% incorrect with six targets.

Although Pylyshyn and Storm (1988) is the paper most frequently cited when a limit of four objects is claimed, even they found a quite gradual decrease in performance (their Figure 1) as the number of targets was increased, from one to five (five targets was the most that they tested). And nowhere in their paper did Pylyshyn and Storm (1988) state that there is a value beyond which performance rapidly declines. Six years later, however, Pylyshyn et al. (1994) did write that it is "possible to track about four randomly moving objects." By 2007, when he published his book *Things and Places: How the Mind Connects with the World*, Pylyshyn wrote sentences like "And as long as there are not more than 4 or 5 of these individuals the visual system can treat them as though it had a concept of 'individual object'" (Pylyshyn, 2007). I suspect that this sort of slide toward seeming to back a hard limit is caused in part by the desire for a simple story. It may also stem from an unconscious oversimplification of one's own data, and/or Pylyshyn's commitment to his theory that tracking is limited by a set of discrete mental pointers.

I have so far addressed only one aspect of the claim (misconception #1): that there is a limit after which performance decreases rapidly. Another aspect of misconception #1 is that the limit is consistently found to be four or five. This isn't viable if there is no limit after which performance decreases rapidly, but a researcher could retreat to misconception #2, the idea that tracking performance falls to some particular level at about four targets, even if this does not mark a hard limit (or even an inflection point). The particular performance level might be 75% correct, or another criterion like the halfway point between ceiling and chance (Holcombe and Chen, 2013), or the "effective number of items tracked," calculated by applying a formula to percent correct with the number of targets and distractors (Scholl et al., 2001). In a charitable reading, this may be what researchers like Alvarez and Franconeri (2007) mean when they write phrases such as: "researchers have consistently found that approximately 4 objects can be tracked" (Intriligator & Cavanagh, 2001; Pylyshyn & Storm, 1988; Yantis, 1992). The early studies cited may indeed be consistent with this statement, albeit not strongly supportive. However, works published over the past fifteen years have revealed this apparent agreement on a soft limit across studies to be an artifact of researchers using similar display and task characteristics. That is, findings that approximately four objects can be tracked based on some performance criterion are just an accident of researchers using similar display parameters.

One of the most important display parameters is object speed. The influence of object speed was demonstrated in dramatic fashion by Alvarez and Franconeri (2007), who tested participants with a display of sixteen wandering discs. When the speed of the discs was very high, participants could, at the end of a trial, correctly pick out the targets only if there were just a few targets. But for very slow speeds, participants could track up to eight targets accurately. This indicated that the accuracy of the statement that participants can track four objects is highly contingent on the speed of those objects. Additional evidence for this was found by others (Feria, 2013; Holcombe and Chen, 2012) and other display parameters that strongly affect the number of objects that can be tracked were also discovered, in particular object spacing (Franconeri et al., 2008; Holcombe et al., 2014).

In summary, it is incorrect to say that people can track about four moving objects, or even that once some (varying with circumstances) number of targets is reached, performance declines very rapidly with additional targets. The number that can be tracked is quite specific to the display arrangement, object spacing, and object speeds. If a researcher is tempted to write that "people can track about four objects," to reduce confusion, I think that they should stipulate that this refers to a particular combination of display characteristics and performance measures.

This issue of how to characterize a human cognitive limit has also bedeviled the study of short-term memory, a literature in which one of the most famous papers is titled "The magical number seven, plus or minus two: Some limits on our capacity for processing information" (Miller, 1956). Two dozen working memory researchers convened in 2013 to highlight empirical "benchmarks" for models of working memory. One issue they considered was how to talk about how many items people can remember. In the paper that they published in 2018, the researchers pointed out that "observed item limits vary substantially between materials and testing procedures" (Oberauer et al., 2018). They suggested, however, that much of this variability could be explained by humans' ability to store groups of items as "chunks," and thus the group endorsed a statement that there is a limit of "three to four chunks" (Cowan, 2001). In the case of short-term memory, then, the observed variability in experiments' results can potentially be explained by a common underlying limit of three to four chunks that manifest as different observed item limits depending on circumstances (in particular, the opportunity for chunking). Evidently there is no simple task parameter unrelated to chunking opportunity, analogous to object speed in the case of MOT, that smoothly varies through a wide range how many items people can remember. However, whether there is an inflection in performance after four objects, or at any point, remains debated (e.g., Robinson et al., 2020).

Another strong candidate for a real capacity limit is the human ability to "subitize" or judge nearly exactly the numerosity of a collection of objects. For this task of reporting how many items are in a briefly presented display, there really does seem to be an inflection point in accuracy when the number of objects shown goes from less than four to more than four (Revkin et al., 2008). Four objects and fewer is frequently referred to as the "subitizing range," with performance approximately as good for rapidly counting four objects as it is for two or one. Note that this is very different than in tracking, for which speed thresholds decline markedly from one to two targets, as well as subsequently to three and four.

In the case of MOT, it remains possible that researchers will be able to identify a set of circumstances that consistently yield a mean tracking limit, in the modal human, of three or four targets if "limit" is defined as performance falling to a particular level on some performance metric. Probably these circumstances will simply be certain spacing, speeds, object trajectories, and number of objects in a display. It would be nice if some underlying construct, the counterpart of memory's "chunks," would be identified to explain how performance changes when other circumstances are used. That would constitute real progress in theory development. However, I don't see much prospect of that based on the current literature.

3.1 Claim #3: Different Tasks, Same Limit?

Even after discarding the idea that there is a particular number of objects that one can track, misconception #3 might still be viable. This claim is frequently tangled up in the myth reviewed above, and sometimes stated as "there is a magical number four." If we discard the idea of a specific number that does not vary with circumstances, there remains the notion that different tasks have the same number-of-objects limit when tested in comparable circumstances. For example, Bettencourt et al. (2011) stated that visual short-term memory and MOT show "an equivalent four-object limit," and Piazza (2010) similarly claimed that visuospatial short-term memory, ultra-rapid counting (subitizing), and MOT, all share a common limit of "three or four items." So far, however, there is no good evidence that object tracking has the same limit as visual working memory and subitizing.

Ideally evidence for a common limit could be found by measuring the limits for all three tasks using the same stimuli, but it is unclear how to equate the information available across tasks. Especially difficult is comparing performance with the briefly presented static stimuli used in subitizing and working memory tasks to the extended exposures of moving stimuli needed to assess object tracking. A stronger understanding of the processes mediating tracking would be required to model performance of the two tasks using a common framework via which they could be compared at an underlying psychological construct level. There is another approach, too: measure the tasks of interest in large numbers of individuals and see whether the different task limits strongly covary between individuals. The relationships found so far are not strong enough to conclude that, however, and they are reviewed in Section 11.

In summary, the idea of a limit of four or five targets is a myth. What's most disappointing is that at no point did it have good evidence behind it, which makes me worry that the way we do science, or the way we do this kind of science, does not result in the community of researchers knowing the basics of what the evidence supports. The general issues around that are beyond the scope of this Element. Let's stick with the facts of tracking and consider the following: given that tracking performance does depend greatly on circumstances and falls gradually rather than displaying a discontinuity at a particular target number, what are the implications for how tracking works?

4 Which Aspect(s) of Tracking Determine Performance?

The number of objects one can track is highly dependent on display characteristics, which hint that the underlying process may be continuous and flexible rather than determined by the fixed, discrete set of pointers hypothesized by Pylyshyn. If so, a person might be able to apply more resource to particular targets to reduce the deleterious influence of a particularly high speed for those targets. There is good evidence for this (e.g., Chen et al., 2013), which will be discussed later, but here I would like to explain the resource concept more, and make an important distinction.

To understand why we can track several objects in some circumstances, but only a few in others, we must distinguish between display factors that impose *data* limitations on tracking and display factors that impose *resource* limitations.

The "data" of data limitation refers to sensory data (Norman and Bobrow, 1975). If a target moving on an unpredictable trajectory moves outside the edge of our visual field, it is the absence of sensory data that prevents tracking. No amount of mental resources can overcome this for an unpredictable stimulus. Data limitations may also occur when sensory signals are impoverished rather than entirely absent. For example, it is a data limitation that prevents tracking when an object travels at such a fast rate that our neurons hardly register it.

People with poor visual acuity perform less well on many visual tasks than people with high visual acuity, due to differences in the sensory data that they have to work with. Thus, some individual differences are almost certainly due to data limitations rather than variation in tracking processes between people. When performance is data-limited, bringing more mental resources to bear provides little to no benefit. The most popular way of investigating this is by varying the number of stimuli one needs to process, as in visual search studies. If the number of stimuli one must evaluate does not affect how well a person can perform a task, this suggests that the task is data-limited rather than resource-limited, because performance is the same regardless of the proportion of the putative resource can be devoted to it.

Resource-limited processing is more interesting for those interested in attention and the capacity limits on mental processing. A classic example is from visual search: if response time or error rate increases with the number of distractors presented, a resource-limited process may be required for success at the task. However, science is hard – an elevation in, for example, error rate can also occur even if there is no resource limitation, if each additional distractor has a non-zero probability of being mistaken for a distractor, yielding more errors with more distractors even if the probability of successfully evaluating each individual stimulus remains unchanged (Palmer, 1995).

Even in ideal conditions, where data limitations are avoided, it will be clear (see Section 5) that the number of objects that can be tracked is much less than the number of objects that are simultaneously processed by early visual areas. In other words, there is some sort of resource limitation.

We'd like to know what factors consume the resource. I'll also be using the term "resource-intensive," meaning a deleterious stimulus factor that can be compensated for by increasing the amount of resource available. One example is the speed of the moving targets. An increase in target speed can hinder performance, but reducing the number of targets can make up for that because it provides more resource to the remaining targets. Moreover, if one object moves faster than another, it consumes more resource. The evidence for that is that the addition of a fast-moving target hurts tracking performance for a first target more than does the addition of a slow-moving target (Chen et al., 2013).

Speed, then, appears to be resource-intensive. Speed also can result in a data limitation, at very high speeds, but long before such speeds are reached, speed is resource-intensive. One should not assume, however, that when one manipulates something about a display, that something is the only thing that changes. Increasing the speed of the objects in a display can also result in more close encounters between targets and distractors, unless one shortens the duration of the trial to equate the total distance the objects travel. Thus, it could be that addressing spatial interference is what consumes resource, rather than speed per se. This brings us to the next section, which is all about spatial interference.

5 Spatial Interference

Details much smaller than ourselves, like the fibers of a sheet of paper, or the individual ink blotches laid down by a printer, are inaccessible to the eye. Visual stimuli that are very close together are experienced as a single unit.

Even when two objects are spaced far apart enough that we perceive them as two objects rather than one, they are not processed entirely separately by the brain. Receptive fields grow larger as signals ascend the visual hierarchy, and this can degrade the representation of objects that are near each other. Such spatial interference is evident in Figure 3.

When gazing at the figure's central dot, you likely can perceive the middle letter to the left fairly easily as a "J." However, if while still keeping your eyes fixed on the central dot, you instead try to perceive the central letter to the right, the task is much more difficult. This spatial interference phenomenon is

O   J   S • O R L H Y M S

Figure 3 When one gazes at the central dot, the central letter to the left is not crowded, but the central letter to the right is

called "crowding" in the perception literature (Korte, 1923; Strasburger, 2014; Wolford, 1975).

Most crowding studies ask participants to identify a letter or other stationary target when flanking stimuli are placed at various separations from the target. How separated the flankers must be to avoid impairment of target identification varies somewhat with the spatial arrangement, but is on average about half the eccentricity of the target, with little to no impairment for greater separations (Bouma, 1970; Gurnsey et al., 2011). Setting the targets and distractors in motion has little effect (Bex et al., 2003), suggesting that these results generalize to tracking – indeed, close flankers not only prevent identification of the target, they can also prevent the target from being individually selected by attention, including for MOT (Intriligator and Cavanagh, 2001).

Crowding happens frequently in typical MOT displays – in most published experiments, objects are not prevented from entering the targets' crowding zones (which as mentioned above, extend to about half the stimulus' eccentricity). It is not surprising, then, that in typical MOT displays, greater proximity of targets and distractors is associated with poor performance (Shim et al., 2008; Tombu and Seiffert, 2008).

5.1 Spatial Interference Does Not Explain Why Tracking Many Targets Is More Difficult than Tracking Only a Few

In 2008, Steven Franconeri and colleagues suggested that spatial interference is the *only* reason why performance is worse when more targets are to be tracked (Franconeri et al., 2008). In the previous section, we introduced the idea of a mental resource that, divided among more targets, results in worse tracking performance. Franconeri suggested that for tracking at least, the only thing that becomes depleted with more targets is the area of the visual field not undergoing inhibition; inhibition stemming from a inhibitory surround around each tracked target (Franconeri et al., 2008, 2013a, 2010). In other words, overlap of the inhibitory surrounds of nearby targets is the only reason for worse performance with more targets, and "there is no limit on the number of trackers, and no limit per se on tracking capacity"; "barring object-spacing constraints, people could reliably track an unlimited number of objects as fast as they could track a single object." Joining Franconeri in making this claim was Zenon Pylyshyn himself as well as other visual cognition researchers, including James Enns, George Alvarez, and Patrick Cavanagh, my PhD advisor (Franconeri et al. [2010], p. 920).

Franconeri et al. (2010) tested their theory by keeping object trajectories nearly constant in their experiments but varying the total distance traveled by the objects (by varying both speed and trial length), on the basis that if close encounters were the only cause of errors, they should be proportional to the total distance traveled. As the theory predicted, performance did decrease with distance traveled, with little to no effect of the different object speeds and trial durations that they used. Franconeri et al. (2010) took this as strong support for the theory that only spatial proximity mattered. However, note that they had varied the potential for spatial interference rather indirectly, by varying the total distance traveled by the objects, rather than simply spacing the objects further apart.

As a more direct test, in 2012 my student Wei-Ying Chen and I used displays in which we could keep the objects widely separated. In one experiment, we created a wide-field display with an ordinary computer screen by having participants bring their noses quite close to it. This allowed us to keep targets and distractors dozens of degrees of visual angle from each other (Holcombe and Chen, 2012). The basic display configuration is shown in Figure 4.

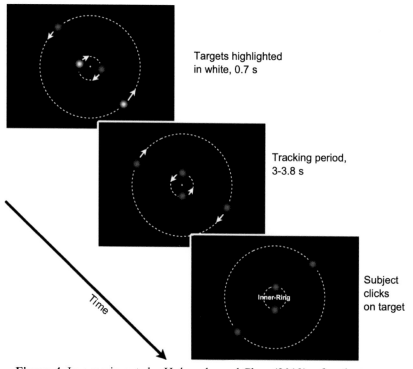

Figure 4 In experiments by Holcombe and Chen (2012), after the targets were highlighted in white, all the discs became red and revolved about the fixation point. During this interval, each pair of discs occasionally reversed their direction. After 3–3.8 s, the discs stop, one ring is indicated, and the participant clicks on one disc of that ring.

Even when all the objects in the display were extremely widely spaced, speed thresholds declined dramatically with the number of targets. To us, this appeared to falsify the theory of Franconeri et al. (2010), that spatial interference was the only factor that prevented people from tracking many targets. In a 2011 poster presentation, entitled "The resource theory of tracking is right! – at high speeds one may only be able to track a single target (even if no crowding occurs)," we suggested that each target, regardless of its distance from other objects, uses up some of a limited processing capacity – a resource that was attentional in that it could be applied anywhere in the visual field, or at least anywhere within a hemifield. The amount of this resource that is applied to a target determines the fastest speed at which a target can be tracked.

Franconeri et al. did not say why they were unconvinced by the findings of Wei-Ying Chen and I, but they took their spatial interference idea much further, suggesting that it could explain the apparent capacity limits on not just tracking, but also on object recognition, visual working memory, and motor control, writing that in each case capacity limits arise only because "items interact destructively when they are close enough for their activity profiles to overlap" (p. 2) (Franconeri et al., 2013a).

To explain the Holcombe and Chen (2012) results, spatial interference would have to extend over a very long distance, farther than anything that had been reported in behavioral studies. If there were such long-range spatial gradients of interference present, it seemed to me that they should have shown up in the results of Holcombe and Chen (2012) as worse performance for the intermediate spatial separations tested than for the largest separations we tested. I made this point in Holcombe (2019), and in reply, Franconeri et al. (2013b) pointed to a neurophysiological recording in the lateral intraparietal area (LIP) of rhesus macaque monkeys by Falkner et al. (2010), who cued monkeys to execute a saccade to a visual stimulus. In some trials a second stimulus was flashed 50 ms prior to the saccade execution cue. That second stimulus was positioned in the receptive field of an LIP cell the researchers were recording from, allowing researchers to show that the LIP cell's response was suppressed relative to trials that did not include a saccade target. This suppression occurred even when the saccade target was very distant – a statistically significant impairment was found for separations as large as 40 deg for some cells.

The data of Falkner et al. (2010) were consistent with the spatial gradient of this interference being quite shallow, allowing Franconeri et al. (2013b) to write that "levels of surround suppression are strong at both distances, and thus no difference in performance is expected" for the separations tested by Holcombe and Chen (2012). One property of the neural suppression documented by Falkner et al. (2010) strongly suggests, however, that it is not one of the processes that limit our ability to track multiple objects. Specifically, Falkner et al. (2010) found that nearly as often as not, the location in the visual field that yielded the most suppression was *not* in the same hemifield as the receptive field center. But as we will see in Section 9, the cost of additional targets is largely independent in the two hemifields. Evidently, then, the suppression observed in LIP is not what causes worse MOT performance when there are more targets. Instead, as Falkner et al. (2010) themselves concluded, these LIP cells may mediate a global (not hemifield-specific) salience computation for prioritizing saccade or attentional targets.

Having failed to find behavioral evidence for long-range spatial interference, my lab decided to focus on the form of spatial interference that we were confident actually existed: short-range interference. Previous studies of tracking did not provide much evidence about how far that interference extended – either they did not control for eccentricity (e.g., Feria [2013]), or they only tested a few separations (e.g., Tombu and Seiffert [2011]).

In experiments published in 2014, we assessed tracking performance for two targets using spatial separations that ranged from within the interference distance documented in crowding studies through to very large separations. Our experiments validated that interference was confined to a short range (Holcombe et al., 2014). Specifically, performance improved with separation, but only up to a distance of about half the target's eccentricity, as is also found for crowding (Strasburger, 2014). In a few experiments there was a trend for better performance as separation increased further, beyond the crowding zone, but this effect was small and not statistically significant. These findings were consistent with our supposition from our previous studies: spatial interference is largely confined to the crowding range. When objects are widely spaced then, the deficit associated with tracking more targets is caused by a limited processing resource.

One result did surprise us: in the one-target conditions only, outside the crowding range, we found that performance *decreased* with separation from the other pair of (untracked) objects. This unexpected *cost* of separation was only statistically significant in one experiment, but the trend was present in all four experiments that varied separation outside the crowding range. This might be explained by configural or group-based processing (Section 8), as grouping declines with distance (Kubovy et al., 1998).

5.2 The Mechanisms That Cause Spatial Interference

As explained in the beginning of this section, one cause of short-range spatial interference is simply poor spatial resolution. If tracking cannot distinguish between two locations, either because of a noisy representation of those locations or because the two locations are treated as one, then a target may be lost when it comes too close to a distractor. This would be true of any imperfect mechanism, biological or man-made. The particular way that the human visual system is put together, however, results in forms of spatial interference that do not occur in, for example, many computer algorithms engineered for object tracking.

Our visual processing architecture has a pyramid-like structure, with local, massively parallel processing at the retina, followed by a gradual convergence to neurons at higher stages with receptive fields responsive to large regions. Processes critical to tasks like tracking or face recognition rely on these higher stages. Face-selective neurons, for example, are situated in temporal cortex and have large receptive fields. For tracking, the parietal cortex is thought to be more important than the temporal cortex, but the neurons in these parietal areas also have large receptive fields.

A large receptive field can be a problem when the task is to recognize an object in clutter or a mechanism to prevent processing of the other objects that share the receptive field, object recognition would have access to only a mishmash of the objects' features. Indeed, this indiscriminate combining of features is thought to be one reason for the phenomenon of illusory perceptual conjunctions of features from different objects (Treisman and Schmidt, 1982). For object tracking as well, isolating the target is necessary to keep it distinguished from the distractors.

In principle, our visual systems might include selection processes that when selecting a target can completely exclude distractors' visual signals from reaching the larger receptive fields. Implementing such a system using realistic biological mechanisms with our pyramid architecture, however, is difficult (Tsotsos et al., 1995). Indeed, while the signals from stimuli irrelevant to the current task are suppressed to some extent, neural recordings reveal that they still have an effect on responses. The computer scientist John Tsotsos has championed surround suppression as a practical way for high-level areas of the brain to isolate a target stimulus. Such suppression likely involves descending connections from high-level areas and possibly recurrent processing (Tsotsos et al., 2008). However, the evidence I have reviewed suggests that these effects are not spatially extensive enough to explain why we can only track a limited number of objects.

The possibility of a suppression zone specific to targets remains understudied, as very few studies of crowding have varied the number of targets. I have found one relevant study, which found that attending to additional gratings within the crowding range of a first grating resulted in greater impairment for identifying a letter (Mareschal et al., 2010). This is consistent with the existence of surround suppression around each target. Unfortunately, however, the study did not investigate how much further, if at all, spatial interference extended when there are more targets.

Although spatial interference in MOT does not extend very far, many MOT experiments involve targets and distractors coming very close to each other, so spatial interference likely contributes to many of the errors in a typical MOT experiment. As we have seen in this section, that may be largely a data limitation – something that occurs regardless of the number of targets, as a result of the inherent ambiguity regarding which is a target and which is a distractor during close encounters for any system with limited spatial resolution; when objects are kept widely separated, it appears that spatial interference plays little to no role in tracking.

Rather than spatial interference, then, something else is needed to explain the dramatic decline in tracking performance that can be found with more targets even in widely spaced displays (Holcombe et al., 2014; Holcombe and Chen, 2012, 2013). The processes underlying this capacity limitation can be described as "an attentional resource," but that doesn't tell us anything about how they work. To gain insight into the tracking processes, we would like to know what specific aspect(s) of tracking become impaired with higher target load. A major clue was provided by Holcombe and Chen (2013), whose experiments revealed that *temporal* interference from distractors becomes much worse when there are more targets.

Temporal interference occurs when a target's location is not sufficiently separated in time from a distractor visiting that location. That is, if distractors visit a location too soon before and after a target has visited that location, people are unable to track. The temporal separation needed increases steeply with the number of targets tracked, approximately linearly according to the evidence so far (Holcombe and Chen, 2013; Roudaia and Faubert, 2017). This is easiest to explain by serial switching models (see Holcombe [2022] for a review). In summary, spatial resolution is not affected much, if at all, by target load, but temporal resolution is. This is our fourth main conclusion about tracking, as was previewed in Section 1.1.

6 Unitary Cognition (System B)

Successful performance of a multiple object tracking task may be assisted by
two resources. One resource is the one that researchers typically believe they
are studying. This resource can process multiple targets simultaneously, even
if it processes them more poorly than it processes a lone target. This is the
resource that most researchers, including myself, use tracking to study. However, the mind also has another resource that likely contributes to tracking
performance.

The processes that support our ability to explicitly reason, often referred to
as System 2 in cognitive psychology, can assist performance in many tasks. But
this system is very limited in capacity – some cognitive researchers think it can
only operate on one thing at a time (Oberauer, 2002). This may be what prevents
us from doing more than one 2-digit mental multiplication problem at a time.
But this also means one can apply System 2 to tracking a single target, for
example, to use what you've learned about object trajectories to predict future
positions. The "System 2" concept was developed within cognitive psychology
to distinguish between two types of cognitive processing. As opposed to the
lower-level processing thought to allow people to simultaneously track multiple
targets, here I want a term that refers to aspects of cognition that have a capacity
of approximately one object. Because I know of no existing term, I will refer
to it with the phrase "System B."

6.1 An Inconvenient Possibility

That tracking performance might reflect a combination of two systems, System
B and a more low-level and possibly higher-capacity tracking process, com-
plicates the interpretation of many experiments. Indeed, it makes the results
trumpeted by some tracking papers fairly uninteresting, because the results
could be caused entirely by our cognitive abilities (System B) operating on
a single target, rather than reflecting the tracking resource that we seem to be
able to distribute to multiple targets. MOT researchers have sometimes con-
tented themselves with showing that a factor makes some non-zero difference
to performance, as if the only criterion for newsworthiness is that the associated p value is less than 0.05. But in a task involving tracking several targets, a
factor that has only a small effect could be explained by System B operating on
just one target. As an example of evidence that such a capacity=1 process may
contribute to visual cognition, Xu and Franconeri (2015) found that participants
could mentally rotate only a single part of a multi-colored shape.

Imagine that a study finds that people track multiple objects more accurately if they move on predictable trajectories than on unpredictable trajectories. This has in fact been found repeatedly, first by Fencsik et al. (2007). Could the result be due to our System B thought processes operating on just one target, rather than it revealing anything about the multiple-object tracking processes? Ruling this out requires sophisticated methods, such as showing that the predictable-trajectory advantage applies independently in each hemifield, as we will see in Section 9, or that the effect shows some other idiosyncrasy of tracking, such as inability to work with individual locations within a moving object, as described in Section 7. Researchers have typically not done this, unfortunately, but what has been done is to assess the capacity limit of the underlying process. The resulting findings suggest that the use of motion information during tracking may be subject to a more severe capacity limit than the use of position. In conditions where participants can use position information to accurately track four or five targets, they can only use motion information for one or two of the targets (Howe and Holcombe, 2012; Luu and Howe, 2015; Wang and Vul, 2021). Perhaps the predictability of trajectories can be taken advantage of only by the extended cognitive processing of an object that System B is capable of.

My essential point is that even when participants are asked to track several targets, one can expect that System B is contributing to overall performance, even if they are only involved in the processing of one of the targets. By using our capacity for reasoning and symbol manipulation, we can perform a wide array of arbitrary tasks, so we should not be surprised by the ability to track a *single* target. We have a visual system that makes the position and direction of motion of objects on our retina available to cognition, and by using our ability to think about where an object is going and deliberately moving our attention to a future anticipated location, we might muddle through to success at tracking a single object. Thus, when researchers contrast tracking performance with different numbers of targets, one reason for the decline in performance may be that System B processes are, in each condition, processing only a single target, so performance declines rapidly with target load.

7 Objects and Attentional Spread

Sunlight streams through the window of my living room, illuminating dozens of objects, including Hugo, our dog, who is lying on his bed in the corner. When Hugo gets up and ambles toward the kitchen, his movement attracts my attention, and I find that I am tracking him, out of the corner of my eye. To accomplish this, something in my brain grouped together a changing set of neurons as a single object as Hugo's image slid across my retinas.

Processing starts in the retina, but further processing in the thalamus and visual cortex is needed to segment an object from the cluttered background presented by my living room. Some of this processing occurs regardless of where one is attending – in other words, it is pre-attentive. Exactly how extensive this pre-attentive processing is, and what sorts of representations it results in, are not fully understood (Kimchi and Peterson, 2008; Neisser, 1963; Treisman, 1964). These preattentive representations are not the same as what we cognitively think of as objects, so one can instead refer to them as proto-objects or use Pylyshyn's term "FING," a play on "thing" and FINST (Pylyshyn, 2001).

It is frequently assumed that pre-attentive processing creates FINGs and attentive tracking simply selects them. This is difficult to investigate directly. What can be studied is which sorts of stimuli can be tracked and which cannot.

7.1 Stationary Object Selection

To access an object, attention may be deployed first to a location or locations, via spatial or featural cuing – while researchers often speak about object-based attention, no one seems to think that objects can be directly selected in the way one can select colors. That is, one cannot think "chair" and expect all the locations of chairs in the scene to rapidly become attended. Selection of chairs and other objects typically requires a search first, using simple features.

After a search yields the location of a target, location selection is possible, but typically we are more interested in an object, an object part, or a surface (Pylyshyn, 2007). So while selection may begin with a location, the presence of something in that location may result in spatial attention spreading throughout it. That likely helps sets the stage for tracking that object. Indeed, if location selection were the only process operating, when an object moved, attention would be left behind. But to me it feels unnatural to un-latch attention from a target and fix it to the target's (former) location while the target moves on. Moving attention with an object seems, in my experience, to take no more effort than attending to a static object. Indeed, attention seems to be positively pulled along – when the targets in an MOT trial begin to move, I have never had the experience of my attention staying behind, remaining at one of the original target locations.

Selection of visual objects has been studied primarily with the paradigm of Egly et al. (1994), in which two static objects (rectangles) are presented, and then a cue is added to one end of an object. The cue can result in performance enhancement not only for probes at the location of the cue, but also at the cued object's other end. The control or baseline condition is typically performance for locations equidistant from the cue but not on the cued object. Most such papers found that participants are fastest and most accurate when the stimulus is presented in the same location as the cue, or on the same object but on a different part of that object. Some papers did not find this (Lou et al., 2020; Davis and Holmes, 2005; Shomstein and Behrmann, 2008; Shomstein and Yantis, 2002), however, and a major concern is that there may be many more such null findings, unpublished and in the file drawer. The effect sizes in the literature are often quite small and the studies not highly powered, which is a red flag that publication bias may have created the illusion of a real effect (Button et al., 2013).

Based on the pattern of sample sizes, effect sizes, and p-values in three dozen published object-based attention studies, Francis and Thunell (2022) argued that publication bias and/or p-hacking in the literature are rife. Substantial proportions of researchers in psychology and other fields admit to such practices (Chin et al., 2021; John et al., 2012; Rabelo et al., 2020), and Francis and Thunell (2022) pointed out that the only published study with a large sample (120 participants) found a non-significant effect, of only a 6 ms response time advantage (Pilz et al., 2012), and in Francis et al.'s own study with 264 participants, the effect was also quite small, at 14 ms. For an effect of this size, Francis et al. calculated that the sample sizes typically used in the published literature were unlikely to yield statistical significance without some help from p-hacking or another questionable research practice. As a result, many papers in the literature make conclusions about objects and attention that unfortunately cannot be trusted.

Publication bias and p-hacking are less of a problem when the effects being studied are large, because in those cases studies are more likely to be adequately powered, resulting in fewer false positives and fewer false negatives. Some effects related to tracking are so large that just seconds of looking at a display is enough to convince oneself that an effect is real. Fortunately, those large effects include some that relate to how variation in objects affects tracking.

7.2 The End of the Line

Many objects have salient parts. For example, the letter "T" is ordinarily considered a single object, but it is made up of a horizontal segment and a vertical segment, which we can easily see. In conscious awareness, then, we have access to both the whole object level and to an individual parts level. You are able to focus attention on individual bits of the vertical segment, even though there are

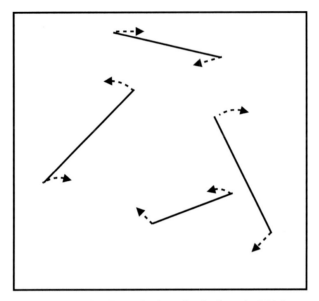

Figure 5 The lines display of Scholl et al. (2001)

no visual characteristics that differentiate it. But what kind of representation(s) does our object tracking processes operate on?

In early visual cortex, different populations of neurons respond to the horizontal and to the vertical stroke of a "T," as well as the different ends of each stroke. But having neurons that respond to a thing is not sufficient for tracking that thing, as tracking operates on only some sorts of representations. Scholl et al. (2001) asked participants to track the ends of lines. While this may seem to be a weird task, it is not entirely artificial. When someone is holding something pointy at close range, for example, it may be important to continuously monitor the location of its front end. Scholl et al. (2001) presented four moving lines in their study (Figure 5), with one end of each line designated as a target. The lines grew, shrank, and rotated as each of its ends wandered about the screen randomly. At the end of the trial, participants were to click with a mouse on the line ends that were targets.

Performance on the task was very poor, including relative to a control condition in which the two ends of the line were not connected. By viewing an example trial (Video 3), one can very quickly get a sense of how difficult the task is.

Howe et al. (2012) showed that various complications in the Scholl et al. (2001) displays, such as that the lines frequency crossed over each other, were not the main reason for the poor performance in tracking the lines' ends. This supported the conclusion that one cannot confine one's tracking processes to

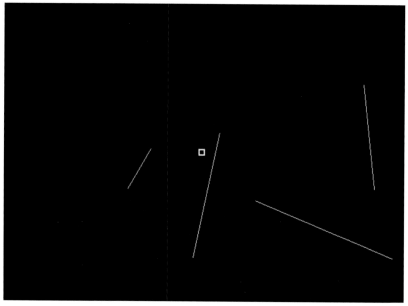

Video 3 Using this display, Scholl et al. (2001) asked participants to track the end of each of several lines. Note: an animated version of the figure is available in the online resources
(www.cambridge.org/Holcombe_supplementary)

one bit of an undifferentiated object. This inability to track line ends fits in with one possibility already mentioned, that preattentive processes define objects, or at least proto-objects (they may not always correspond to what we consciously think of as objects), and this is what tracking operates on. Consistent with this, maintaining attention on a part of the visual scene in the absence of anything in the image to delineate that part feels like it requires concentration, as if we must continually think about what we are supposed to be attending to. If cognitive "System B" is indeed needed to maintain the "object" representation when it is not provided by preattentive processes, then for such objects we may only be able to track one (this idea that processes with a capacity of 1 are involved or required for some forms of tracking was introduced in Section 6).

7.3 Object Creation and Object Tracking: Distinct Processes?

Researchers typically make a strong distinction between the processing that determines *how many* objects one can track and those that determine *what kinds* of objects can be tracked. Such an assumption of separate processing stages is popular in the study of visual cognition quite generally. Visual search, for example, is usually conceptualized this way (Nakayama et al., 1995; Wolfe and Bennett, 1997), and a two-stage theory appears to be implicitly assumed in two previous reviews of objects and tracking (Pylyshyn, 2006; Scholl, 2001). It would be quite convenient if the assumption that object creation and object tracking occur at distinct processing stages were true, as that is more straightforward to study than an interactive system (Simon, 1969; Sternberg, 1969).

It is unclear whether processing is actually neatly divided, with preattentive representations simply selected. Instead, attention may modify or even create the representation that is tracked (see Figure 6). It is possible that the feature binding role of attention does not affect tracking, but attention may contribute more directly to figure-ground segregation, which is fundamental to objecthood (Peterson, 2014).

Maechler et al. (2021) found evidence that tracking operates on perceived (illusory) object positions, which suggests that tracking operates on high-level representations. Nevertheless, attention and object creation may be interactive. The way stimuli are organized by attention can determine what illusory contours, lightness, and depth are perceived (Harrison and Rideaux, 2019; Harrison

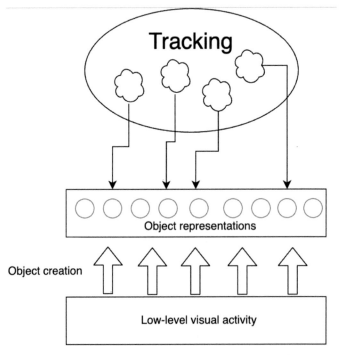

Figure 6 A schematic of the idea that objects are created prior to the action of tracking processes, which then point to the already-formed object representations but do not change them

et al., 2019; Peter, 2005). Our ability to perceive the complex motion of a human body from sparse points of light highlights that object perception can involve an interaction between Gestalt grouping and top-down knowledge of the relative motion pattern of their parts (Johansson, 1973; Wang et al., 2010) (see Section 8). Further evidence for a role for neural feedback in object segmentation comes from Ongchoco and Scholl (2019), who asked participants to practice imagining a shape in a uniform grid of lines until they felt they could actually see the shape. Participants were able to do this fairly readily, and the detection of flashed probes was higher for probes presented on the same imagined object compared with equidistant ones presented on different objects.

The same attentional resources that mediate tracking may also contribute to the creation of object representations. One consequence would be a trade-off between the involvement of attention in constructing object representations and the number of objects that can be tracked. Informal experience with tracking the line ends in the Scholl (2001) display seems to support this. If when you watch Video 3, you concern yourself with keeping track of the end of only *one* object, you are likely to succeed. But recall that it is difficult or impossible to accurately track *four* object ends – indeed, Scholl (2001) found that participants' performance was approximately that predicted if they could track one line end, but not more. It is unclear whether the ability to track one line end is due to the use of multiple-object tracking resources to create objects, or rather reflects System B processing that has a capacity of only one object.

Involvement by System B could mean that covert tracking of a single object is qualitatively different from covert tracking of multiple objects. Because the participants in the Ongchoco and Scholl (2019) study imagined only a single object, it is possible that their results reflect a capacity-one process rather than the processes we use to track multiple objects.

7.4 What Tracking Sticks To

Even when all our attentional resources, System B included, are brought to bear on a single entity, some entities still can't be tracked. In the "chopsticks illusion," a horizontal and vertical line slide over each other, with each line following a clockwise circular trajectory. Viewers perceive the intersection of the two lines to also be moving clockwise, but in fact the intersection moves counterclockwise only, and participants cannot track the intersection accurately with their eyes (Anstis, 1990). Covert object tracking also seems to be impossible, because if one was able to attentionally track the intersection, presumably one would know whether it was moving clockwise or counter-clockwise.

The true counterclockwise trajectory of the chopsticks' intersection becomes obvious perceptually if one views the display through a window so that the ends of the lines are occluded rather than visible. In that condition, participants were able to follow the intersection accurately with their eyes. These results suggest that the illusion-evoking configuration is interpreted in a way we cannot overcome, and that interpretation occurs prior to the operation of tracking, even though what is to be tracked is a rather simply-defined point – an intersection. Anstis (1990) suggested that the reason that the intersection is perceived to move in the wrong direction is because the clockwise motion of the ends of the lines is mistakenly assigned to the intersection, similar to how visibility of the ends of lines can veto the barber-pole illusion (Wuerger et al., 1996). This is consistent with Figure 6, which portrays motion and form processing occurring prior to the operation of tracking.

As discussed previously, maintaining and using a representation of an undifferentiated part of an object is not something that our multiple object tracking processes are capable of. So, what differentiation of object parts is needed in order to track? This is not yet clear. Scholl et al. (2001) and Howe et al. (2012) found seemingly contradictory evidence for how distinct the ends of a dumbbell figure had to be from its center to allow tracking of the dumbbell end. That may reflect the noisiness of the data of the two studies. Howe et al. (2012) also tested a "luminance" condition (Figure 7); performance (80% correct) was substantially lower than their baseline condition (96% correct), although not as low as for undifferentiated bar ends (72% correct). The clear difference in luminance between the targets and the connector in the luminance condition was somehow not enough to keep tracking from being so adversely affected by the connectors. This reinforces the notion that multiple object tracking uses a different representation of objects than what is available when we focus our attention on a single object.

What we consciously experience also seems to differ from the object representation operated on by visual search processes. Wolfe and Bennett (1997)

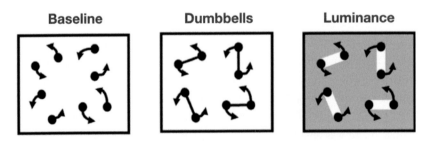

Figure 7 Some stimuli from Howe et al. (2012), CC-BY

asked participants to search for conjunctions of features, such as red and vertical. When the vertical red part of an object was physically connected to a horizontal and green part, participants were much slower to find the red vertical target segment in the display, among the green vertical and red horizontal distractors. Physically connecting one feature to another evidently lumped them together as an undifferentiated collection of features, what Wolfe and Bennett (1997) termed a "preattentive object file." Unfortunately, no researcher seems to have tested displays of this nature for both tracking and search. For now the parsimonious account is that multiple object tracking and search operate on the same object representations.

7.5 Growth, Shrinkage, and Tracking

Some objects and substances change their shape as they move. A bathroom faucet, for example, will shoot a jet of water down into the sink, whereupon the water flattens on the sink's bottom as it expands into a puddle. When beer is poured by a bartender, a froth forms, which gradually thickens as the top of the liquid rises. The froth and beer as they fill the glass, as well as the water emanating from the faucet, is an example of non-rigid, shape-shifting motion.

VanMarle and Scholl (2003) concocted a stimulus that moved a bit like an inchworm. In what I will refer to as their "slinky" condition, each of the target and distractor objects began as a square. The object (a slinky) moved by extending its leading edge until it had the shape of a long and thin rectangle. Subsequently, the trailing edge of the slinky, which was still at its original location, would move forward until the slinky was a square again, now entirely at a new location. Performance was very poor in this task.

What causes the difficulty of tracking slinkys? Knowing that should tell us something about how tracking works. Howe et al. (2013) tested a number of conditions that help rule out various possibilities, such as the faster speed of the slinky's edges relative to the non-slinky objects. Scholl (2008) purport to provide one explanation, writing that "there was no unambiguous location for attention to select on this shrinking and growing extended object" because "each object's location could no longer be characterized by a single point" (p.63). There may be something to this, but it is not entirely clear what Scholl (2008) mean by an object's location not being characterizable by a single point. The objects typically used for MOT, uniform discs, also have no unambiguous internal locations – their insides are a completely undifferentiated mass. As a single point to represent their locations, the objects' centroid could be used, but this seems just as true for an object changing in size and shape like the slinky.

A further problem is that in the chopsticks illusion discussed earlier, the target was defined by a single point (the intersection of two lines), yet it could not be tracked.

One clue to the mystery is that both tracking and simple localization are disrupted by object expansion and contraction, which is one characteristic of slinky motion. After Howe et al. (2013) replicated the tracking findings of Scholl (2008), they went on and probed the effect of size changes on localization. Participants were presented with a rectangle for 200 ms at a random location on the screen, and were asked to click on the location of the center of the rectangle. In a baseline condition, the rectangle did not change in size, shape, or location during its 200 ms presentation. In the size-change condition, the length of the object increased due to expansion for half of the interval and shrank due to contraction during the other half. Participants' localization errors were about 14% larger in this changing-size condition. This appeared to be driven by errors along the axis of the object's expansion and contraction, as errors in the orthogonal direction were not significantly different from the baseline condition.

The substantial localization impairment documented by Howe et al. (2013) may be the cause of the poor performance during MOT. An important next step is to measure localization errors when the task is to monitor multiple objects changing in size rather than just one. If the localization deficit caused by change in size worsens with object load, this would help implicate the processes underlying tracking. This would not by itself answer, however, why exactly object localization is impaired by size changes.

7.6 Could Tracking Work by Attentional Spreading?

I don't recall anyone suggesting that the manner in which attention selects object representations might also facilitate tracking an object as it moves. However, this seems quite possible. Object selection may begin with selection of a particular location on that object, with attention subsequently spreading up to the edges of the object. Neurophysiological evidence for this has been observed in some tasks (e.g., Wannig et al., 2011). This spreading of attention may contribute to the ability to track – when the object moves, its leading edge will occupy new territory while its trailing edge continues to occupy an old location. If attentional spread up to object boundaries continues to occur as the object moves, then attention should spread to the newly occupied locations at the leading edge. Thus attention could follow a moving object. One should also not overlook the possible contribution of the fact that visual transients attract attention – a moving object is essentially a rapid sequence of transients that appear along a path.

The spreading account seems to predict that tracking resources would be most concentrated near the trailing end of an object. In a task involving tracking multiple lines, however, Alvarez and Scholl (2005) found that probes presented at the center of objects were detected much more accurately than end probes, suggesting that attentional resources were concentrated near the centers of the lines. It appears, however, that Alvarez and Scholl (2005) did not analyze the data to check whether of the two object ends, accuracy was higher for probes at the trailing end. Clearly, more work is needed to reveal the nature of attentional spread while an object moves and any role that may have in facilitating tracking.

8 Grouping

Carving the scene into objects is not the only segmentation challenge our visual systems solve. Our visual brains also provide us with an experience of groups of objects. Can tracking operate over groups, allowing us to track multiple groups of objects? Alzahabi and Cain (2021) attempted to investigate this using clusters of discs as targets and as distractors. These clusters maintained a constant spatial arrangement as they wandered about the display. Participants seemed to do well at tracking these clusters. However, the associated experiments did not rule out the possibility that participants were tracking just one disc of each cluster. I am not aware of any work providing good evidence that a tracking focus can track an entire group.

Yantis (1992) hypothesized that during MOT experiments, participants track an imaginary shape formed by the targets, specifically a polygon whose vertices are the target positions. This became a popular idea, but progress has been slow in understanding whether all participants do this or just a minority do, and in what circumstances. Merkel et al. (2014) found a result that they took as evidence that some participants track a shape defined by the targets. In their task, at the end of the trial when the targets and distractors stopped moving, four of the objects were highlighted. The task was to press one button if all four were targets (match), and to press a different button otherwise (non-match). Error rates were lowest when none of the objects highlighted were targets, and errors were progressively more common as the number of highlighted objects that were targets increased. This was unsurprising. For trials where all four of the highlighted objects were targets (match), however, error rates were much lower than when only three were targets (a non-match). Merkel et al. (2014) suggested that this reflected a "perceptual strategy of monitoring the global shape configuration of the tracked target items." They went on to split the participants based on whether they had a relatively low error rate in the match condition, investigated the neural correlates of that, and drew conclusions about the neural processing that underlies virtual shape tracking.

The inferences of Merkel et al. (2014) are based on the split of participants based on low error rate in the match condition compared to the condition where none of the highlighted objects match. The idea seems to be that if participants weren't using a shape tracking strategy, error rates would steadily increase from the trials where none of the highlighted objects were targets to the trials where all of the objects highlighted were targets. While this is not necessarily the case, it does seem likely that participants use the shape to rapidly classify the trial as match or non-match. People can certainly see shapes defined only by dots at their vertices; the ancients saw animals and human figures in the stars. Subitizing, a related ability that involves processing several objects as a group, allows one to enumerate a collection much faster than by considering individual dot positions. So using shape is indeed a natural way to check for a match. However, it is harder to know how much grouping contributes to the ability to track.

In addition to their behavioral measures, Merkel et al. (2017) also measured the electrical brain response (the evoked response potential or ERP) to a probe that was flashed while the objects were moving. The probe was flashed either directly on the virtual outline shape formed by the targets, outside that shape, or inside it. The participants were not informed of the probe and most reported not being aware of it. However, the early ERP response to the probe (~100 ms) was significantly greater when it lay on the shape than outside it or inside it. By 200 ms, the response to the probe when inside the virtual outline shape was similar to that on the virtual outline, and greater than when the probe was outside the shape. This suggests that at least some of the participants were continuously tracking the shape. The source of the ERP shape advantage was localized to around the lateral occipital complex, which is known to be particularly involved in shape processing. Future work ought to test with probes in both hemifields to assess whether this virtual shape grouping occurs independently in both hemifields, as it should if it is to explain our capacity for tracking.

Representing moving objects by the virtual shape they define is merely one way that position representations may be configural rather than retinotopic. A few studies speak to this issue by manipulating the stability of different coordinate frames, and find evidence for non-retinotopic processing; I point to papers on this in the "Omissions" part of Section 13.

8.1 Hierarchical Relations

In the real world, the movement of object images on our retinas is rarely as independent as the movement of the objects in an MOT experiment. In everyday scenes, often there is a strong motion element throughout the visual field created by the movement of the observer, and recovering true object movement involves detecting deviations from that overall motion (Warren and Rushton, 2007). Even when the observer and their eyes do not move, hierarchical motion relationships are common. When one views a tree on a windy day, the largest branches sway slowly, while the smaller limbs attached to the larger branches move with the larger branches but also, being more flexible and lighter, have their own, more rapid motion.

These aspects of the structure of the visual world may be one reason that our visual systems are tuned to relative motion (Maruya et al., 2013; Tadin et al., 2002). When we see a wheel roll by, we experience individual features on the wheel as moving forward, reflecting the global frame of the entire wheel, but also as moving in a circle, reflecting the motion relative to the center of the wheel.

This decomposition of a wheel rim's movement is so strong that people systematically mis-report the trajectory of the points on the wheel (Proffitt et al., 1990). The red curve in Video 4 reveals that a point on a rolling wheel follows a trajectory with up, down, and forward motion, but no backward motion. Yet people report that they see a circular trajectory, including backward motion. What we perceive, then, reflects a sophisticated parsing and grouping of retinal motion.

Bill et al. (2020) varied the motion pattern of the discs of an MOT task to show that hierarchical relations in the stimulus can facilitate tracking. Unfortunately, they did not investigate whether those relations affected how the discs' motion was perceived, like in a rolling wheel or a flock of birds. The attentional demands, if any, of such hierarchical motion decomposition has not been explored much. Thus it remains unclear to what extent the hierarchical relations

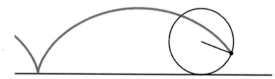

Video 4 The red curve is that traced out by a point on a rolling wheel, by Zorgit https://commons.wikimedia.org/wiki/User:Zorgit. Note: an animated version of the figure is available in the online resources (www.cambridge.org/Holcombe_supplementary)

are calculated by the application of tracking or other attentional resources, versus tracking operating on a representation of hierarchical relations that was determined pre-attentively.

8.2 Eyes to the Center

The human visual system performs a rapid global analysis of visual scenes, providing summary information sometimes referred to as "ensemble statistics" (Alvarez and Oliva, 2009). One such ensemble statistic is the location of the center or centroid of a set of objects. This is useful for eye movement planning, among other things – to monitor a group of objects, it is helpful to look at the center of the group, as that can minimize how far into peripheral vision the objects are situated.

Zelinsky and Neider (2008) and Fehd and Seiffert (2008) both reported that during multiple object tracking, the eyes of many participants frequently are directed at blank locations near the center of the array of targets. This finding has been replicated by subsequent work (Hyönä et al., 2019). The nature of the central point that participants tend to look at (in addition to the individual targets, which they also look at) is not entirely clear. Researchers have suggested that the point may be the average of the targets' locations, or the average location of all the moving objects (both targets and distractors). Another possibility that has been investigated is that participants tend to look at the centroid of the *shape* formed by the targets, which recalls the Yantis (1992) hypothesis that what is tracked is the shape defined by the targets. Lukavský (2013) introduced the idea of an "anti-crowding point," which minimizes the ratio between each target's distance from the gaze point and distance from every distractor. The idea was that participants move their gaze closer to a target when it is near a distractor to avoid confusing targets with distractors. Note, however, that the Lukavsky metric does not take into account the limited range of the empirical crowding zone, which is about half the eccentricity of an object.

In a comparison of several metrics against the eyetracking data, Lukavský (2013) found that the anti-crowding point best predicted participants' gaze in his experiment, followed by the average of the target locations. These points both matched the data better than the centroid of the targets. This undermines the Yantis (1992) hypothesis that a virtual polygon is tracked, and the finding of best performance for the anti-crowding point is consistent with other results that participants tend to look closer to targets that are near other objects (Vater et al., 2017; Zelinsky and Todor, 2010).

More work must be done to understand the possible role of the anti-crowding eye movement strategy suggested by Lukavský (2013). Spatial interference does not seem to extend further than half an object's eccentricity, in both static identification tasks (Pelli and Tillman, 2008, Gurnsey et al. [2011]) and multiple object tracking (Holcombe et al., 2014), but the anti-crowding point devised by Lukavský (2013) does not incorporate such findings. Its performance should be compared to a measure that is similar but excludes from the calculation distractors further than about half an object's eccentricity.

9 Two Brains or One?

A human brain has two halves, a left and a right, that are anatomically connected, but there are fewer cross-hemisphere connections than there are within-hemisphere connections. Much of sensory and perceptual processing runs rather independently in the two halves of the cortex, but more cognitive functions such as declarative memory benefit from a tight integration. This integration is extensive enough that the comparison of our two hemispheres to our two hands or our two legs is misleading.

Our conscious experience, too, is quite unified. We experience no discontinuity when the movement of our eyes, or of an object, cause an object to shift from one hemifield, where it is processed predominantly by one hemisphere, to the other hemifield. Communication between the two hemispheres happens rapidly and continuously. The claims of those who prey on well-meaning schools and parents, there is no good evidence that exercises designed to insure both hemispheres process stimuli have any benefit for learning.

In "split-brain" patients, many of the connections between the hemispheres have been lost. Such patients can still perform tasks such as visual search in both hemifields, suggesting that both hemispheres have the mechanisms needed to do the tasks. When split-brain patients are asked to search for a target among many distractor objects, spreading the load by distributing the distractors across the two hemifields can yield a large benefit, suggesting that the two hemispheres in these patients carry out their searches independently (Luck et al., 1994). For intact individuals, no such advantage is seen, suggesting that in a normal brain, the processes that evaluate each stimulus for whether it is the target are integrated across the hemispheres into a single attentional focus (Luck et al., 1989).

Although the two hemispheres work as one during many tasks, each hemisphere does specialize in certain functions. The left hemisphere has greater competence in language functions such as reading, while the right hemisphere is better at recognizing faces. One behavioral consequence is that response times for a face recognition task are slightly faster when the stimulus is presented wholly in the left hemifield (to the right hemisphere) than when it is presented wholly in the right hemifield, whereas the opposite is found for word reading (Rizzolatti et al., 1971). With extended time to process a stimulus, however, such behavioral asymmetries can disappear, because eventually the information from one hemisphere gets communicated to the other.

From the performance of most perceptual and attentional tasks, then, in typically developing humans there is little overt sign that the brain is divided into two halves. Multiple object tracking, however, is a major exception to this. The pattern of performance found indicates that the limited resource that determines how many objects one can keep track of resides largely with processing that operates independently in the two hemispheres.

9.1 The Extraordinary Hemifield Independence of Object Tracking

In 2005, George Alvarez and Patrick Cavanagh reported a stunning MOT finding. They used objects that resembled spinning pinwheels, and they designated individual bars of the different pinwheels as targets. Performance in a two-target condition was contrasted with a one-target condition (Alvarez and Cavanagh, 2005). When the second target was positioned in the same hemifield as the first target, accuracy in the two-target condition was much worse than in the one-target condition (89% vs. 63%). Remarkably, however, when the second target belonged to a pinwheel located in the *opposite* hemifield, there was very little performance decrement – accuracy was 93% in the one-target condition, and 90% correct in the two-target condition. This suggests that the processes that limit successful tracking in this task are specific to each hemifield.

It was already known that sensory processing and quite a lot of perceptual processing occurs independently in each hemisphere. What is interesting here is that a higher-level, limited-capacity process would be hemisphere-independent. Such capacities were traditionally thought to be among the processes that are tightly integrated across the two hemispheres, forming a single resource "pool," not two independent limits. We will get back to this point, but first we'll examine more extensively the evidence for hemispheric independence of object tracking.

9.2 Quantitative Estimates of Independence

The hemispheric independence of a task, such as MOT, can be quantified. Imagine that adding a second stimulus to a hemifield reduces performance by

20 percentage points, but adding that stimulus to the other hemifield reduces performance by only 5 percentage points. One can quantify the hemispheric independence, then, as $(20 - 5)/20 = 75\%$ hemifield independence. Ideally, however, one would not use raw accuracy but instead would correct for the accuracy one can achieve by guessing. When applying such a calculation to the Alvarez and Cavanagh (2005) results, the estimated level of independence is very high: 88% independence in one of their experiments, and 92% in the other.

Alvarez and Cavanagh (2005) themselves, like others who have studied this issue, did not do these calculations. Alvarez and Cavanagh (2005) calculated expected performance if the hemifields are in fact completely independent, and reported that performance was not statistically significantly worse than that figure, and suggested on that basis that there is complete hemifield independence. That, however, is the fallacy of concluding a null hypothesis is true when the evidence does not reject it at a $p<.05$ level (Aczel et al., 2018). This is not uncommon in the scientific literature – setting the null hypothesis to the desired conclusion (complete independence), and then affirming this conclusion on the basis of not finding much evidence against it. Nevertheless, the data of Alvarez and Cavanagh (2005) do suggest (with unknown confidence, because the uncertainty was not quantified) a hemispheric independence level of approximately 90%. In a study with similar methods, Hudson et al. (2012) found 65% independence (this is my calculation).

Some of the follow-up studies in this area have not included enough conditions to quantify the degree of independence, or confounded distribution of the targets to two hemifields with greater distance among them, such that any benefit might have been due to less spatial crowding interference, a phenomenon discussed in Section 5. Holcombe and Chen (2012) and Chen et al. (2013), however, also found evidence for a high degree of independence, using a slightly different approach based on speed thresholds. The findings were compatible with 90–100% hemifield independence. Shim et al. (2010) and Störmer et al. (2014) also found evidence for a substantial bilateral advantage compared to having two targets in the same hemifield.

The findings of hemispheric independence have not replicated in all circumstances (e.g., Shim et al., 2008) but the balance of published evidence strongly suggests that at least in some circumstances, tracking does occur mostly independently in the two hemispheres. I say "mostly independently" rather than suggesting complete independence because each individual study has too much statistical uncertainty to rule out a figure such as 75% independence, even for the point estimates I've reported above that suggest a higher degree of independence.

Shim et al. (2008) suggested that the reason they did not find evidence for hemifield independence is that they used only two targets; according to them, the original Alvarez and Cavanagh (2005) report of hemifield independence used four targets. This is unlikely to be the reason for the discrepancy, however, because in their E1 and E2 Alvarez and Cavanagh (2005) did find evidence for hemifield independence using just two targets, as did Holcombe and Chen (2012) and Störmer et al. (2014). The Shim et al. (2008) data may have been afflicted by a ceiling effect, as accuracy was over 85% correct in all conditions in their experiment.

A limitation of deriving hemispheric independence from accuracy is that it depends on the assumption that if a person can only track one target, in a condition where the person is also trying to track a second target the person will succeed just as often in tracking one of the two. My introspective experience, however, indicates that in some circumstances, trying to track both targets causes one to fail at both, and thus one is better off only trying to track one. A particular threshold amount of resource is needed to track a target, and so if neither target is allocated that much resource, tracking will fail for both. Evidence for this was provided by Chen et al. (2013). In the terminology of the Norman and Bobrow (1975) framework introduced in Section 4, this would be described by saying that the resource function that relates attentional resource proportion to accuracy falls below a straight line. One implication is that quantitative estimates of hemispheric independence will be overestimates, particularly in circumstances where the participants do not realize they may be better off focusing their efforts on tracking fewer targets than the number they have been told to track .

Carlson et al. (2007) found evidence not only for hemifield independence but also for quadrant-level independence, which they attributed to the partial anatomical separation of the retinotopic quadrant representations in areas V2 and V3. Using different stimuli, Shim et al. (2008) and Holcombe et al. (2014) did not, however, find evidence for quadrantic independence. More work on this topic is needed.

9.3 Some Tracking Resources Are NOT Hemifield-specific

One attentional process that is *not* hemifield-specific is feature attention, for example attention to color. When a participant is told to look for a red target, they are able to use feature attention to enhance all red objects, no matter where they are in the visual field (White and Carrasco, 2011). The decision to look for red originates with cognitive processes and remains hemifield-unified rather than hemifield-specific at the level of visual cortex (Saenz et al., 2002). Indeed, people seem to be unable to confine the enhancement of red objects to one hemifield (Lo and Holcombe, 2014). In real-world tracking where objects are at least somewhat heterogeneous and thus targets often have a different average color and other features than distractors, feature attention will facilitate tracking, and this facilitation is not hemifield-specific.

Section 6 introduced the idea of C=1 cognitive processes that can support tracking of a single target but perhaps not multiple targets. Such processing likely is not hemisphere-specific, being aligned with "central executive" processes that integrate processing in both hemispheres.

Chen et al. (2013) found evidence for both hemifield-specific tracking processes and also processes not specific to a hemifield, operating in the same MOT task. Two targets were used, and on some trials they moved at different speeds. When a slow-moving target was paired (presented in the same trial) with a speedier target, accuracy was lower for the slow-moving target than if it was paired with a target that was slower. This suggests that participants allocate more tracking resources to the faster of two targets, presumably because slower targets do not require much resource to track well. This trade-off was most pronounced when the two targets were in the same hemifield, but seemed to occur to some degree even when the two targets were in different hemifields, implicating a cross-hemifield resource that plays a small role. This cross-hemifield resource may be a C=1 process. Furthermore, as discussed in the next section, perturbing one parietal lobe can affect performance in both hemifields, which suggests that each hemisphere can in some circumstances mediate tracking in either hemifield.

9.4 The Underlying Mechanisms

The evidence reviewed above for hemifield independence suggests that hemisphere-specific processes determine how many targets one can track. This raises the question of what sort of processes those are, and how they interact with the cognitive processes that are more integrated across the hemispheres.

Steve Franconeri and colleagues have championed the idea that the hemisphere independence stems from spatial interference processes; they suggested that spatial interference occurs largely within a hemisphere (Franconeri, 2013). The idea is that when an object is tracked, the neurons representing that target in retinotopic cortical areas activate inhibitory connections to nearby neurons, suppressing the responses to neighboring objects. To explain the findings of hemifield specificity, an important detail of the account is that the inhibitory neural connections do not extend from one hemisphere's retinotopic map to another (Franconeri et al., 2013a). This is plausible because in classic crowding tasks, spatial interference does show a discontinuity across the left- and right-visual field boundary (Liu et al., 2009). However, Holcombe et al. (2014) found evidence against spatial interference extending any further than the classic crowding range of half the eccentricity of an object (for which an object placed six degrees of visual angle from where the point the eyes are looking at would be interfered with only by other objects closer to it than three degrees of visual angle (Bouma, 1970)). Because in most studies of hemifield independence, the stimuli are not close to the vertical midline, any modulation of the crowding range by the vertical midline would not yield apparent evidence of hemifield independence, contrary to the hypothesis of Franconeri et al. (2013a). The more viable theory of hemifield independence, then, is that of two neural resources that span each hemifield.

Consistent with a putative pool of attentional resources, a number of studies have found that the activity of some parietal and frontal areas of cortex increase steadily with the number of targets in MOT (Alnaes et al., 2014; Culham et al., 2001; Howe et al., 2009; Jovicich et al., 2001; Nummenmaa et al., 2017). Unfortunately, these studies provided little information about whether these activations are specific to target load within a hemifield, so we cannot be sure whether the brain activation measured reflects the hemifield-specific resource or a more global resource. The only imaging study I am aware of that investigated the issue is Shim et al. (2010), who did find an activation difference when the objects designated as targets were in opposite hemifields compared to when they were in the same hemifield. The activation difference was found for the superior parietal lobule and transverse parieto-occipital area, suggesting that they may be part of the hemifield-specific resource. The difference was not found for the anterior intraparietal sulcus, which could mean its activation reflects a global resource.

Störmer et al. (2014) used electroencephalography (EEG) to investigate the hemifield-specific resource. SSVEP activation for targets was higher than that for distractors, especially when the two targets were positioned in different (left and right) hemifields. In contrast, an event-related potential (ERP) component known as the P3 thought to reflect more cognitive identification and decision processes was similar in the two conditions. This is consistent with the theory that tracking depends on hemisphere-specific attentive processing followed by some involvement of higher-order processes that are not hemisphere-specific.

Battelli et al. (2009) found they could disrupt MOT performance in a hemifield by stimulating the contralateral intraparietal sulcus (IPS) via repetitive transcranial magnetic stimulation. Importantly, this only occurred when the moving targets were present in both hemifields. When the targets were all in the left or all in the right hemifield, TMS to the left or to the right IPS had no effect on tracking accuracy, a result that replicated in a second experiment. This phenomenon is reminiscent of the inter-hemifield competition evident in "extinction," a symptom seen in parietal neglect patients.

In extinction, responding to stimuli in the hemifield contralateral to parietal injury is only impaired if there are also stimuli presented to the ipsilateral hemifield. This, together with the analogous finding from tracking and TMS, inspired Battelli to propose two things. The first is that the IPS in each hemisphere can mediate the tracking of targets in *either* visual hemifield. The second is that under normal conditions, inter-hemisphere inhibition reduces the ipsilateral processing of each IPS, causing tracking capacity to be effectively hemifield-specific.

Evidence from patients and MOT also suggests a complicated relationship between the hemispheres. Battelli et al. (2001) found that in patients with damage to their right parietal lobe, MOT performance in the left visual field only was impaired, as expected – the right parietal lobe does not normally mediate tracking in the right visual field, so losing it did not hurt right visual field tracking performance. For an apparent motion task, however, the right parietal patients had impairments in *both* hemifields. The suggested involvement of the right parietal lobe, but not the left parietal lobe, in judging apparent motion and the temporal order of stimuli in *both* hemifields, which was further supported by an additional study with patients and TMS study (Agosta et al., 2017).

In summary, while there is evidence that parietal cortex is involved in field-wide processing for some tasks, it also likely mediates the hemifield independence evident in some circumstances. Both aspects may be in operation when a target travels from one hemifield to another. Using ERP, Drew et al. (2014) found evidence that when a target crosses the vertical midline, say from the left to the right hemifield, the left hemisphere becomes involved shortly before the target reaches the right hemifield, and the right hemisphere remains involved for a short time after the crossing. Because this was modulated by predictability of the motion, it did not appear to be entirely mediated by the well-known overlap of the two hemispheres' receptive fields at the midline. This phenomenon may reflect the normally inhibited ipsilateral representation of the visual field by parietal cortices highlighted by Battelli et al. (2009), although this remains uncertain as the origin of the ERP signals was not clear.

Consistent with tracking being mediated largely by the contralateral hemisphere, both Strong and Alvarez (2020) and Minami et al. (2019) found evidence for a tracking performance cost when a target in MOT crossed the vertical midline. In a memory paradigm, too, Saiki (2019) found evidence that when two objects moved between hemifields, memory for their features was more disrupted than when they moved from one to another quadrant within the same hemifield. Similarly, Strong and Alvarez (2020) found no cost when targets moved between quadrants while remaining within a hemifield, an important finding given that other work raised the prospect of quadrant-specific resources (Carlson et al., 2007).

In summary, areas of parietal cortex likely subserve the hemifield-specific tracking resource that determines MOT capacity, but also may provide a resource that is not hemifield-specific. As we will see in Section 10, the hemifield-wide process may be responsible for feature updating and binding.

9.5 What Else Are Hemifield-specific Resources Used For?

Multiple object tracking may involve the same spatial selection process as that used to select stimuli in popular attentional tasks, which use static stimuli almost exclusively. Is spatial selection even with static stimuli, then, hemifield-specific? Decades ago, performance for static stimuli tasks had been compared when two stimuli are presented in the same hemifield to when the stimuli are presented in different hemifields. For example, Dimond and Beaumont (1971) found that reporting two briefly presented digits is associated with higher accuracy when the digits are presented in different hemifields than in the same hemifield. However, that study and others of that era did not include a single-stimulus condition, so for the higher performance in the split condition, we don't know how close it is to the one-target level of performance, and therefore we can't calculate the magnitude of the different-hemifield advantage. Moreover, many studies used response time as a measure, which can be difficult to interpret quantitatively (Awh and Pashler, 2000; Dimond and Beaumont, 1971; Sereno and Kosslyn, 1991).

For a proper assessment of hemifield specificity in a visual working memory task, Delvenne (2005) used both dual-target and single-target conditions, and calculated 40% hemifield independence. Unfortunately, however, he used the discredited A' measure of performance (Zhang and Mueller, 2005) and did not space the stimuli widely enough to reduce the possibility of spatial interference (crowding). Nevertheless, the advantage was large and did not occur for non-spatial color working memory (Delvenne, 2012). This latter finding is one example of a broader result that has emerged, that only tasks with spatial demands seem to show a substantial different-hemifield advantage (Holt and Delvenne, 2015; Umemoto et al., 2010).

Alvarez et al. (2012) studied visual search, with the stimuli to search arrayed bilaterally or unilaterally. In a standard search task, they found only a small advantage of the bilateral display. In a subset search task where participants knew the target would be located in one of several locations designated by a pre-trial cue, however, they found a large bilateral advantage. When the relevant locations were visually salient (due to a color difference) rather than requiring top-down selection, the bilateral advantage largely disappeared. These results, and those reviewed above, suggest that hemifield advantages are strongest when spatial selection is critical.

Finally, Strong and Alvarez (2020) investigated spatial working memory for stimuli that moved either within a hemifield or between hemifields. For between-hemifield movement, they found a substantial decrease in accuracy for remembering which positions of a 2x2 grid contained dots at the beginning of the trial, before the (empty) grid moved – 79% correct for between-hemifield movement, and 85% correct for within-hemifield movement. This between-hemifield cost for spatial memory was similar to the cost they found for MOT itself. No such cost was found for color or identity memory tasks.

The association found between spatial tasks and a different-hemifield advantage may reflect a large-scale difference in how the brain processes spatial versus identity information. Famously, the dorsal stream is more concerned with spatial information than is the ventral stream, which is more involved in object recognition (Goodale and Milner, 1992). Neural responses in the dorsal pathway to parietal cortex are largely contralateral (Sereno et al., 2001), although as we have seen above, this may depend on having stimuli in both hemifields. Contralateral dominance is also found for other brain areas thought to contribute to a "saliency map" (Fecteau and Munoz, 2006), such as the frontal eye fields (Hagler Jr and Sereno, 2006), the superior colliculus (Schneider and Kastner, 2005), and the pulvinar (Cotton and Smith, 2007). In contrast, identity-related processing seems to involve more bilateral neural responses and connectivity between hemispheres (Cohen and Maunsell, 2011; Hemond et al., 2007).

The multiple identity tracking (MIT) task, which is discussed further in Section 10, combines the location-updating demand of multiple object tracking with an additional requirement to maintain knowledge of what features belong to each of the objects. Across four MIT experiments, Hudson et al. (2012) consistently found partial hemifield independence for this task, ranging from 26 to 37% (my calculations are here) with a paradigm that yielded 65% independence for MOT. This is consistent with the suggestion of the findings listed above that spatial selection and/or location updating processes are much more hemisphere-specific than processes that require maintenance of non-spatial features.

Putting it all together, spatial selection appears to occur at a hemifield-specific stage, with other features subsequently updated and linked in at a field-wide stage.

9.6 Hemispheric Differences

So MOT and spatial selection seem to be limited by processing that happens concurrently and independently in the two hemispheres. Are the two hemispheres doing exactly the same thing?

Any functional differences between the left and right cerebral hemispheres if often attenuated at the behavioral level by the cross-hemisphere integration that can occur. But tracking processes, or at least the processes that underlie tracking capacity, work independently in the two hemispheres, and thus there is a higher potential to show hemifield differences than for other tasks. As it turns out, however, while some differences have been observed, they do not seem to be large.

In each of four experiments conducted for a 2014 paper, my colleagues and I found either a trend for or a statistically significant advantage for targets in the right hemifield (Figure A2) (Holcombe et al., 2014). This was also found by Strong and Alvarez (2020). Interestingly, there was some non-significant evidence that this was greater in their one-target condition than in their two-target condition. Figure 4 of Battelli et al. (2001), like Holcombe et al. (2014), shows better tracking performance in the RVF than the left only when tracking one target, although this finding was also not statistically significant.

The right hemifield advantage, if it replicates, could be explained by the idea that stimuli presented to the right hemifield are processed by both hemispheres to a greater degree than are stimuli presented to the left hemifield. This is a leading explanation of why left neglect is more common than right neglect – the right hemisphere is thought to mediate attention to *both* hemifields (Mesulam, 1999), such that the right hemifield is doubly processed. However, while Strong and Alvarez (2020) did find a right hemifield advantage in their MOT experiments, they found a *left* visual field advantage for spatial working memory experiments, even though spatial working memory is also thought to be mediated by parietal cortex. Most strikingly, Matthews and Welch (2015) found a large advantage for temporal order judgments and simultaneity judgments for stimuli presented to the left hemifield, which may reflect specialization by the right parietal cortex (Battelli et al., 2003).

The situation becomes more complex when one considers that subtle interactions between the two hemispheres seem to affect attention in each hemifield, as highlighted above in the "The Underlying Mechanisms" subsection. A recent finding by Edwards et al. (2021) illustrates this. Participants were trained on MOT in a hemifield for 30 min, and afterwards there was little to no accuracy change in the trained hemifield, but a significant performance improvement was found in the *untrained* hemifield. The reason for this is not clear, but could reflect "fatigue" by the hemisphere contralateral to the trained hemifield and an associated reduction of its inhibition of the other hemisphere. Alternatively, the mechanism could be potentiation (an increase in gain) of the untrained hemisphere as a result of the deprivation, which may be the reason why depriving an eye results in increased cortical activity when that eye is stimulated later (Lunghi et al., 2011).

10 Knowing Where but Not What

Imagine a friend visiting a museum, says that they are trying to keep track of their family members. What do they mean by that? They might mean that they are continuously aware of where each of their children are, and their spouse. They probably also mean that they are keeping track of which of them is where. The laboratory MOT task, however, does not assess participants' awareness of which target is where – participants report where the targets are, but do not indicate which is which.

This illustrates that there are two important questions about the role of object identities in tracking. The first is how the position updating aspect of tracking works – does it use differences between the distractors' and targets' features to help keep track of the targets? The second question is the extent to which the features of targets are available to conscious awareness – do we know what we are tracking?

10.1 The First Question: Does Position Updating Benefit from Differences in Object Identities?

10.1.1 Motion Correspondence

In industrial settings, algorithms track objects to detect intrusions and threats to safety. In sports, tracking algorithms analyze how the players on a team move relative to each other, and in animal labs they monitor the movements of study subjects. Engineers who develop such algorithms do not confine themselves to using only the locations and motions of objects – they also use the appearance of those objects, for example their shapes and colors. This facilitates matching objects across video frames (known as the correspondence problem, or in engineering as the "data association problem") (Yilmaz et al., 2006).

The fact that object features are useful for tracking does not necessarily mean that the brain uses them. The division of cortical visual processing into two streams, dorsal and ventral, hints that it might not. The dorsal "where" pathway specializes in motion and position processing, leaving much of object recognition to the ventral stream (Goodale and Milner, 1992). This division may help explain why position updating does not seem to involve much processing of objects' other features.

The Gestalt psychologist Max Wertheimer found that apparent motion was equally strong whether the objects in successive frames had different features or identical features (Wertheimer, 1912). Later studies found that featural similarity has some effect, but still only a small one (Burt and Sperling, 1981; Kolers and Pomerantz, 1971), so the dominant view today is that the visual system does not use feature similarity for motion correspondence to update a moving object's position. Some caution is appropriate, however, because when the successive presented frames of an object touch or overlap with each other rather than being presented in non-contiguous locations, the results can be different. In such "line motion" or "transformational apparent motion" displays, feature similarity, especially contour continuity, but also color, can determine which tokens are linked together perceptually (Faubert and Von Grunau, 1995; Tse et al., 1998). Thus, feature similarity *can* be involved in motion processing, even though in many situations motion correspondence is instead almost completely determined by spatiotemporal luminance patterns. An important characteristic of this process that does not seem to have been studied is whether the more complex cues documented by Tse et al. (1998) and others are processed in parallel. Short-range spatiotemporal luminance relationships ("motion energy," roughly) are processed in parallel, by local detectors, yielding parallel visual search for a target moving in an odd direction defined by small-displacement apparent motion (Horowitz and Treisman, 1994). I am not aware of any studies that have investigated this for transformational apparent motion, in a situation where the perceived motion direction is determined by feature similarity. Thus, the possibility remains that feature similarity effects are driven by a capacity-one process, what I have called System B (Section 6).

10.1.2 Feature Differences, but Not Feature Conjunction Differences, Benefit Tracking

While motion correspondence is usually driven only by spatiotemporal luminance information, object featural information can benefit position tracking via the action of feature attention. Attention can select stimulus representations by their color, so that one can, for example, enhance the selection of all red objects in the visual field. Makovski and Jiang (2009) confirmed that this process can benefit MOT. They used eight moving objects, four of which were targets. MOT performance was better when the eight objects were different in color than when they were identical. This was also true when the objects were all different in shape.

Apart from the usefulness of attending to an individual feature when the targets differ in that feature from the distractors, do feature differences otherwise benefit tracking? A large body of evidence has supported Treisman's theory that feature pairing information, in contrast to individual features, does not efficiently guide attention to targets (Treisman and Gelade, 1980; Wolfe, 2021). Consistent with this, Makovski and Jiang (2009) found that targets having unique feature pairings do not benefit tracking performance. In their "feature conjunction" condition, each object had a unique pair of features, while it shared the individual features with at least one other object. Performance was no better in this condition than if the objects were all identical. It is this pairing situation that prevents featural attention from contributing, and the results suggest that the tracking process itself does not use featural differences.

10.2 The Second Question: Are We Aware of the Identities and Features of Objects We Are Tracking?

10.2.1 Feature Updating

A common view among lay people may be that we are simultaneously aware of the identities of all the objects in the central portion of our visual field, so unless an object actually disappears, hides behind something or someone, or moves to the edge of our visual field, we should always know where everything in the scene is, and we should readily detect any changes to these objects.

Change blindness demonstrations expose how impoverished our ability to detect changes is. They typically use stationary objects, and associated experiments indicate that although people cannot simultaneously monitor a large number of objects for change, they are able to monitor several, perhaps four or five (Rensink, 2000). People seem to do this by loading selected objects into working memory and then, in the second frame of a change blindness display, checking whether any are different than what is held in memory.

The ability to load into memory the features of objects for storage and subsequently compare them to a new display with the objects in the same location may have different demands than continuously updating awareness of the changing features of objects. It appears that hundreds of milliseconds are needed to encode several objects into memory (Ngiam et al., 2019; Vogel et al., 2006). Without a visual transient to call attention to the site of a change, then, the brain is easily overwhelmed by the task of updating the features of the objects in a typical scene. This is even more true of scenes with moving objects, because motion means continuous transients, masking the transient caused by a featural change.

An example of the failure to detect changes to even a limited number of moving objects was provided by Saiki (2002), who had participants view a circular array of colored discs that rotated about the center of the screen. Occasionally discs swapped color when they briefly went behind occluders, and the participants' task was to detect these color switches. Performance decreased rapidly with disc speed and number of discs, even though the motion was completely predictable, and Saiki (2002) concluded that "even completely predictable motion severely reduces our capacity of object representations, from four to only one or two." Because we now understand that simple MOT does not work well across occluders, however, that interpretation of the study is limited by the absence of an MOT-type control. However, the finding was taken further by Saiki and Holcombe (2012) without occluders, using a field of 200 moving dots. In one condition, half were green and half were red and the task was to detect a sudden change in color of all the dots. Even when all 200 dots simultaneously switched color between red and green, performance in detecting the switch was very poor. Why had such a dramatic change blindness phenomenon never been noticed before? The phenomenon only occurred when the relative proportion of the two colors was approximately the same before and after the switch, indicating that what is sometimes called "summary statistics" for the overall display are updated readily, but individual pairings of dots with colors are not. This phenomenon was made into an even more dramatic demonstration by Suchow and Alvarez (2011). A full explanation of the phenomenon continues to be debated, but I think it makes it clear that non-position feature updating is less likely to occur with a moving object than with stationary objects. For a stationary object, a feature change will typically stimulate motion/transient detectors, drawing attention to the change and triggering an update. Not so with moving objects, as the motion detectors are continually stimulated, so a feature change does not yield an attention-drawing transient.

Even when objects are stationary, featural updating can be slow. Howard and Holcombe (2008) investigated feature updating by having Gabor targets continually change in orientation or spatial frequency. After a random interval of this continuous change, all the objects disappeared and the location of one was cued – the task was to report its last feature value. Participants tended to report an earlier feature value for the object than its value on the last frame, as one would expect due to either a feature integration time or intermittent updating. What was more interesting was that this lag increased with the number of objects monitored. In the spatial frequency condition, the lag was approximately 140 ms when monitoring one Gabor, 210 ms for tracking two Gabors, and 250 ms for tracking four Gabors. The lags increased also for monitoring orientation and for monitoring location, although not nearly as much: 1 orientation = no measurable lag, 2 orientations = 10 ms, and four orientations = 40 ms, and for position 40 ms, 50 ms, and 90 ms. It's possible that a position cue, which may be updated more in parallel, contributed to the orientation reporting. If the objects were put in motion, it is possible that performance and the effect of target load would be even worse, but to my knowledge this has never been investigated. The results of some other behavioral paradigms also point to feature updating being sluggish (Callahan-Flintoft et al., 2020; Holcombe, 2009).

Overall, these results suggest a very limited-capacity system is required for updating some features, whereas position updating seems less capacity-constrained. One might hope that even with a very limited-capacity system of feature updating, however, that simple *maintenance* of the features of objects as they move could easily be done. Instead, maintenance of tracked targets' identities can be very poor, as we will see in the next section.

10.2.2 Maintenance of Target Features and Identities

According to Zenon Pylyshyn's FINST (Fingers of Instantiation) theory of tracking, a small set of discrete pointers are allocated to tracked targets. Pylyshyn's idea was that a pointer allows other mental processes to individuate and link up with an object representation, and the pointer's continued assignment to a target facilitates representing the corresponding object as the same persisting individual (Pylyshyn, 1989). This implies that when tracking multiple targets, people should know which target is which. However, when Pylyshyn tested this, the results turned out differently than he expected. The first of two papers he wrote on the topic was entitled "Some puzzling findings in multiple object tracking: I. Tracking without keeping track of object identities." Targets were assigned identities either by giving them names or by giving them distinct and recognizable starting positions: the four corners of the screen (Pylyshyn, 2004). Participants were given the standard task of indicating which objects had been designated as targets, but also were asked about the identity of the target – which one it was. Accuracy at identifying which target was which was very low, even when accuracy reporting their positions was high. However, the task was always to report all the locations first and report the identities second, raising the possibility that the need to remember the identities for longer could have contributed to the poorer performance.

More evidence for a disconnect between knowledge of what one is tracking and success at the basic MOT task was found by Horowitz et al. (2007), who had participants track targets with unique appearances - the stimuli were cartoon animals in one set of experiments. At the end of each trial, the targets moved behind occluders so that their identities were no longer visible. Participants were asked where a particular target (say, the cartoon rabbit) had gone - that is, which occluder it was hiding behind. This type of task had been dubbed "multiple identity tracking" by Oksama and Hyönä (2004). Performance was better than chance, but was worse than the standard MOT task of reporting target locations irrespective of which target a location belonged to. This basic finding was replicated in four additional experiments. The effective number of objects tracked, as reflected in a standard MOT question, was around three or four, but for responses about the final location of a particular animal, capacity was estimated as closer to two objects. So, the evidence seems robust that knowledge of which target is which is often poor, in contrast to Pylyshyn's original view that this information was part and parcel of the tracking mechanism.

A counterpoint is that Wu and Wolfe (2018) found only a fairly small performance deficit for identity reporting relative to position reporting. Using MOT and MIT tasks carefully designed to be comparable, they had participants track 3, 4, or 5 targets, and found 96%, 89%, and 86% accuracy for the MOT task, against 93%, 85%, and 79% accuracy for the MIT task. While the high performance for the 3-target condition could be a ceiling effect, that is probably not the case for the 4- and 5-target conditions. One difference with previous work is that at the beginning of a trial, all the stimuli (cartoon animals) were stationary and participants had unlimited time to memorize the targets' locations. When a participant was ready, they would press a key and the animals transformed into identical gray circles and began moving. At the end of the trial, one of the circles was probed and the participant either had to indicate whether it was a target, or indicate whether it had originally been a particular animal. One possible explanation of the discrepancy with previous findings is that while identities are not native to tracking's pointers in the way Pylyshyn thought, with adequate time for memorization the associations can be made and maintained.

10.2.3 Beaten by a Bird Brain

Pailian et al. (2020) investigated identity maintenance during tracking in a format like a hustler's shell game. The engaging nature of the shell game format made it suitable for testing children and an African grey parrot as well as human adults (Figure 8).

Figure 8 An African grey parrot participates in the shell game used by Pailian et al. (2020). CC-BY Hrag Pailian

As stimuli, Pailian et al. (2020) used colored wool; real balls of wool, actually, not pictures on a screen. Between one and four of the balls were shown to a participant, after which the experimenter covered the balls with inverted plastic cups, and with their hands swapped the positions of first one pair, then another. After a variable number of swaps, the experimenter produced a probe ball of one of the target colors, and the task was to point to (or peck on, in the case of the parrot), the cup containing the probed color.

I would have predicted that people would be able to perform this task with high accuracy, especially given that not only were only two objects in motion at any one time, the experimenter paused for a full second between swaps, which ought to give people sufficient time to update their memory of the locations of those two colors. When only two balls were used, accuracy was in fact high: over 95%, even for four swaps, which was the highest number tested. This was true for the human adults, the parrot, and the 6- to 8-year-old children alike.

In the three-ball condition, the adults did fine when there were only a few swaps, but their performance fell substantially as the number of swaps increased, to about 80% correct for four swaps. For some reason, participants did not reliably update the colors for four swaps. The effect of number of swaps was more dramatic for the children. They performed near ceiling for the zero-swap (no movement) condition, but accuracy fell to close to 80% in the one-swap condition, and to around 70% for two and three swaps.

Remarkably, the parrot actually outperformed not only the children, but also the human adults. It seems that this was not due to more practice – the authors state that the parrot learned the task primarily by simply viewing the experimenter and a confederate perform three example trials (the parrot was experienced with a simpler version of the task involving only one object presented under one of the three cups). That the bird had the ability to remember and update small sets of moving hidden objects to a level of accuracy similar to humans, despite having a brain less than one-fiftieth the size.

What needs to be explained is why the Harvard undergraduates, who almost surely had above-average intelligence and motivation, displayed levels of accuracy that were not very high when there were more than a few swaps. Prior to the publication of this study, I had assumed that the reason for poor performance in multiple identity tracking was the difficulty of updating the identity of three or four targets simultaneously while they moved. I would have predicted that changing positions exclusively by swapping the positions of just two objects, with a one-second pause between swaps, would keep performance very high. These results, then, suggest that updating the memory of object locations is quite demanding. Thus, not only does identity updating not happen automatically as a result of object tracking, but also it may rely on a very sluggish memory updating system.

Another reason many should be surprised is the popularity of the "object files" idea that all the features of an object are associated with a representation in memory, the object file, that is maintained even as an object moves (Kahneman et al., 1992). In associated experiments, a trial begins with a preview display with two rectangles. Each rectangle contains a feature – usually a letter. The letter disappears, and the rectangles move to a new location. The observer's representation of the display is then probed by presenting a letter once again in one of the rectangles, or elsewhere, and asking participants to identify it. If the letter is the same as the one presented in that rectangle at the beginning of the display, observers are faster to respond than if it had appeared in another rectangle in the beginning of the display, indicating that aspect of the rectangle's initial properties was maintained, with its location updated. One difficulty with interpreting this response time priming phenomenon is that, because responses must be averaged over many trials to reveal it, we do not know on what proportion of trials it is effective. Thus it is hard to know whether it is inconsistent with the behavioral findings mentioned above that show successful updating on only a minority of trials.

There is also the question of the capacity of the object-file system: whether several object files could easily be maintained and updated. Kahneman et al. (1992) found that the amount of priming was greatly diminished when four letters were initially presented in different rectangles, suggesting that fewer objects than that had letter information maintained and updated. They concluded that there may be a severe capacity limit on object files or object file updating. The evidence from the studies in this section overall suggests that identity updating is very poor in a range of circumstances.

10.2.4 Some Dissociations between Identity and Location Processing Reflect Poor Visibility in the Periphery

To explain why participants don't update the identities of tracked moving objects nearly as well as they update their positions, the Finnish researchers Lauri Oksama and Jukka Hyönä suggested that identities are updated by a serial one-by-one process, while positions are updated in parallel. Oksama and Hyönä were motivated by evidence from eye tracking. During an MIT task, Oksama and Hyönä (2016) found that participants frequently looked directly at targets, for more than 50% of the trial duration, and frequently moved their eyes from one target to another. In contrast, during MOT, the participants moved their eyes infrequently, and their gaze wasn't usually at any of the moving objects, rather they were more often looking somewhere close to the center of the screen. Oksama and Hyönä (2016) took these results to mean that the targets' identity-location bindings that must be updated during MIT are updated by a serial one-by-one process, whereas target positions during MOT are updated by a parallel process; for a review, see Hyönä et al. (2019).

A problem for interpreting the Oksama and Hyönä (2016) results is that participants may have had to update target identity information one-by-one purely due to limitations on their peripheral vision. That is, the targets (line drawings) likely were difficult to identify when in the periphery. Thus, participants may have had to move their eyes to each object to refresh their representation of which was which. Indeed, in a subsequent study, Li et al. (2019) tested discriminability of the objects in the periphery and found that accuracy was poor. When colored discs were used as stimuli instead of line drawings, accuracy was higher in the periphery and participants did not move their eyes as often to individual targets, which suggests at least some degree of parallel processing, leaving the amount of serial processing for simple colors, if any, in doubt.

Many findings of differences between MIT and MOT performance may be explained by poor recognition of the targets in the periphery. One could blur the objects to impair localization but it is not clear what degree of spatial uncertainty is comparable to a particular level of object identifiability; an apples-and-oranges problem.

One dissociation between identity and location tracking performance seems to remain valid regardless of the difficulty of perceiving object identities in the periphery. This is the original finding by Pylyshyn (1989), replicated by Cohen et al. (2011), that if targets are actually identical but are assigned different nominal identities, participants are very poor at knowing which is which at the end of the trial because in this paradigm, there is no visible identity information.

10.2.5 Evidence from Two Techniques Suggests Parallel Updating of Identities

Howe and Ferguson (2015) used two techniques to investigate the possibility that serial processes are involved in multiple identity tracking. First, Howe et al. applied a simultaneous-sequential presentation technique that when applied to MOT had yielded evidence for no serial processing (Howe et al., 2010a). In the technique, the stimuli are presented either all at once (simultaneously) or in succession (sequentially). In the successive condition, half the stimuli were presented in the first interval of a trial, and the other half in the second interval. If a serial process is required to process each stimulus, the prediction is that performance should be better in the sequential condition, as the presentation duration of each stimulus is equated for the simultaneous and successive conditions, but in the simultaneous condition a one-by-one process wouldn't have enough time to get through all the stimuli. The technique has been applied extensively to the detection of a particular briefly presented alphanumeric character among other briefly presented alphanumeric characters, and researchers have found that processing in the simultaneous condition is equal to or better than the sequential condition, suggesting that at least four alphanumeric characters can be recognized in parallel (Hung et al., 1995; Shiffrin and Gardner, 1972).

As an MIT simultaneous-sequential paradigm, Howe and Ferguson (2015) presented four targets of different colors moving among four distractors. Each of the four distractors was the same color as one of the targets, so that the targets overall could not be distinguished from the distractors by color. In the simultaneous condition, all the objects moved for 500 ms and then paused for 500 ms, a cycle that repeated throughout the trial. In the sequential condition's cycle, half the targets moved for 500 ms while the other half were stationary, and subsequently the other half of targets moved for 500 ms while the others remained stationary. Performance was similar in the simultaneous and sequential conditions, supporting the conclusion that there was no serial process required for the task (Howe and Ferguson, 2015). This conclusion is limited, however, by an assumption that any serial process could respond efficiently to the movement cessation of half the targets by shifting its resources to the moving targets, while not causing any forgetting of the locations and identities of the temporarily stationary targets. To support this assumption, Howe and Ferguson (2015) pointed out that Hogendoorn et al. (2007) had shown that attention could move at much faster rates than 500 ms per shift. However, the Hogendoorn et al. (2007) studies did not assess the attention shifting time between unrelated targets, rather their shifts were for attention stepping along with a single target disc as it moved about a circular array. Thus, it is unclear how much the results of Howe and Ferguson (2015) undermine the serial, one-by-one identity updating idea embedded in the theories of Oksama and Hyönä and Lovett et al. (2019).

Howe and Ferguson (2015) further investigated serial versus parallel processing in MIT by using another technique: systems factorial technology (Townsend, 1990). The two targets were presented in the same hemifield, to avoid independence by virtue of the hemispheres' independence (Alvarez and Cavanagh, 2005). The participants were told to monitor both moving targets and that if either darkened, to press the response button as quickly as possible, after which all the disks stopped moving and the participant was asked to identify the location of a particular target, for example the green one (the objects were identical during the movement phase of the trial but initially each was shown in a particular color). To ensure that participants performed the identity tracking task as well, only trials in which the participant reported the target identity correctly were included in the subsequent analysis. Detection of the darkening events was very accurate (95% correct). On different trials, either both targets darkened, one of them darkened, or neither of them darkened, and each could darken either by a small amount or by a large amount. The pattern of the distributions of response time for the various conditions ruled out serial processing (if one accepts certain assumptions), implicating limited-capacity parallel processing. This suggests that participants can process luminance changes of two moving targets in parallel while also maintaining knowledge of the identity of the moving targets. One reservation, however, is that it is unclear how often the participants needed to update the target locations and refresh their identities, because the rate at which they needed to be sampled to solve the correspondence problem is unclear for the particular trajectories used (this issue is explained in Holcombe [2022]). It also would be good to see these techniques applied to targets defined only by distinct feature conjunctions, with no differences in features between the targets and the distractors. This would prevent any contribution of feature attention, and with processing of feature pairs likely to be more limited-capacity than that of identifying individual features, the results might provide less evidence for parallel processing.

10.3 Eye Movements Can Add a Serial Component to Tracking

Partially in response to the evidence of Howe and Ferguson (2015) against serial processing in tracking, Oksama and Hyona, with Jie Li, revised their Model of Multiple Identity Tracking (MOMIT) to add more parallel processing. MOMIT 2.0 states that the "outputs of parallel processing are not non-indexed locations but proto-objects that contain both location and basic featural information, which can be sufficient for tracking in case no detailed information is required" (Li et al., 2019). This is a reasonable response to the evidence, even if it unfortunately means the theory doesn't make as strong predictions, as the role of serial processing is now more vague. In this model, serial processing is tied to eye movements and is used to acquire detailed visual information for refreshing working memory representations. The theory seems to be mute on whether serial processing would be involved if both fixation were enforced and the stimuli were easily identifiable in the periphery.

Let's step back and consider the role of eye movements in everyday behavior. People move their eyes about three times a second, partly because it is usually adaptive to direct the fovea at whatever object we are most interested in. Rarely are all visual signals of interest clustered together enough that they can be processed adequately without moving the fovea among them. Finally, animals like ourselves have drives to explore visual scenes, because we evolved in complex and changing environments. Perhaps, then, one should expect frequent eye movements to occur even when they are not strictly necessary.

Eye movements usually contribute a serial, one-by-one component to processing, because high-resolution information comes from only a single region on the screen – the region falling on the fovea. People are cognitively lazy in that they seem to structure eye movements and other actions in tasks so as to minimize short term memory requirements (Hayhoe et al., 1998). Even when saccading to different targets is inefficient because people can keep information in memory, and update information in the periphery, people may move their eyes anyway. The most interesting evidence for serial processing, then, may be that found when eye movements are prohibited. The steep decrease with load of apparent sampling rate discovered by Holcombe and Chen (2013) constitutes some evidence for that.

To summarize this section, both use of object identities in tracking and the updating of target identities for awareness are typically poor. This fits with broader findings over the past thirty years that the mind maintains fewer explicit visual representations than we intuitively believe but quick attentional deployment to tracked locations means that the world can serve as an outside memory for content (O'Regan, 1992).

11 Abilities and Individual Differences

For studying tracking, so far we have discussed only the classic experimental approach of manipulating different factors within participants. This has led to our present understanding of the roles of spatial interference, temporal interference, and some of the relationships to the processes underlying other tasks. However, a different approach, the study of individual differences, is also valuable. In the individual-differences approach, the pattern in scores on different tests is examined to see which abilities tend to go together in the natural variation between humans. Those abilities that co-vary the most are more likely to share many processes in common than those that don't.

11.1 Do People Vary Much in How Many Objects They Can Track?

Generally in psychology, documenting a difference among people requires more than ten times as many participants as a within-participants experimental design (Schönbrodt and Perugini, 2013), but some studies have failed to use large samples. In addition to this shortcoming of the literature, there are also two other common pitfalls of MOT and MIT individual-difference studies.

One pitfall is not considering that differences in motivation can explain certain individual-difference findings. Meyerhoff and Papenmeier (2020) tested fifty participants and for each calculated the effective number of items tracked, for a display with four targets and four distractors. The modal effective number of items tracked was around two, but a substantial proportion of participants came in at three targets or one target tracked, and a few scored close to zero items tracked. Meyerhoff and Papenmeier (2020) concluded that some participants could only track one or zero targets, while others can track more. Unfortunately, however, there is no way to know how much of the variation between individuals is due to motivation rather than ability. Measuring motivation reliably is very difficult, but researchers can include attention checks or catch trials to facilitate exclusion of participants who show clear evidence of not reading the instructions carefully, or frequently not paying attention.

Oksama and Hyönä (2004) were also interested in how many objects people can track. They managed to test over two hundred participants, and like Meyerhoff and Papenmeier (2020) they found what appeared to be a substantial variation in capacity, with some people able to track six objects, while many could track only two or even just one. Their participants, who were provided by an air pilot recruitment program, were made up entirely of those who scored in the top 11% on intelligence test scores from a larger group. This provides some confidence that the participants were motivated. The study, however, suffers from what I think of as the second pitfall – the failure to assess task reliability. On any test, a participant will tend to get somewhat different scores when tested on two different occasions, even if they did not learn anything from their first experience with the test. The extent to which participants' scores are similar when taking a test twice is known as test-retest reliability. Ideally, this is measured with two tests administered at very different times, but a more limited assessment is provided by dividing a single session's trials into two groups and calculating the correlation between those two groups, which is known as split-half reliability. Knowing the reliability can allow us to calculate how much of the variation in scores between participants is expected based on the noisiness of the test. Without knowing the reliability, there remains the possibility that the extreme variation in scores, with some participants' data indicating that they could only track one target, could be due to limited reliability – extensive testing of these participants might reveal that their low score was merely a fluke.

Subsequent studies have assessed reliability. Happily, the reliabilities they have found for MOT are very high – 0.96 (Huang et al., 2012), 0.85 (Wilbiks and Beatteay, 2020), 0.92 (Treviño et al., 2021), and 0.87 (Eayrs and Lavie, 2018), near the highest of all the tests administered in the studies (although only the split-half measure was calculated rather than testing on separate days). This looks especially good when one considers that many basic cognitive and attentional tasks have notoriously low reliabilities (Hedge et al., 2018). Tasks with low reliabilities are not well suited for individual-differences studies – as mentioned above, individual-difference studies are largely based on measuring the pattern of correlations between tasks to reveal the relationship among abilities. The lower the reliability of a task, the harder it is to reliably measure the correlation with another task.

What do these high reliabilities mean for tracking? It suggests that the large individual differences observed by Oksama and Hyönä (2004) and others are actually real. Possibly, some young, healthy, high-intelligence people can truly only track one target. Second, the high task reliability of MOT means that individual-difference studies are a viable avenue for gaining new insights about tracking and its relation to other mental abilities.

In the general population, ageing is likely a major source of individual differences in MOT – older participants perform much worse than younger participants (Roudaia and Faubert, 2017; Sekuler et al., 2008; Trick et al., 2005). Using a task requiring participants to detect which of multiple objects changed its trajectory, Kennedy et al. (2009) found a steep performance decline between 30 and 60 years – the effective numbers of trajectories tracked in a multiple trajectory tracking task dropped by about 20% with each decade of aging, and the researchers found that this could not be explained by a drop in visual acuity. This is something that theories of aging and attention ought to explain. This result must also color our interpretation of individual-difference studies using samples with a wide age range – some of the correlations with other tasks will likely be due to those abilities declining together rather than them being linked in people of the same age. That's still useful for drawing inferences, but the inferences should perhaps be different than from individual-difference studies of undergraduates.

The MOT individual difference literature has mostly taken a fairly wide-angle approach. Participants have been tested with a variety of tests, to see which mental abilities are linked. However, the first large-scale study concentrated on tasks typically thought of as attentional (Huang et al., 2012). Liqiang Huang and his colleagues used tests of conjunction search, configuration search, counting, feature access, spatial pattern, response selection, visual short-term memory, change blindness, Raven's test of intelligence, visual marking, attentional capture, consonance-driven orienting, inhibition of return, task switching, mental rotation, and Stroop. In their sample of Chinese university students many of these tasks showed high reliabilities of over 0.9, meaning that there was a potential for high inter-task correlations (inter-task correlations are limited by the reliabilities of the two tasks involved). However, the highest correlation of a task with MOT was 0.4. That task was counting, which required judging whether the number of dots in a brief (400 ms) display were odd or even (3, 4, 13, and 14 dots were used, so the task included the subitizing range). Change blindness, feature access, visual working memory, and visual marking were runner-ups with correlations with MOT of around 0.3.

That no task had a higher correlation than 0.4 is very interesting, but also disappointing. It's interesting because it suggests that MOT involves distinct abilities from several other tasks that have previously been lumped together with MOT as being "attentional." It's disappointing because it suggests that our theoretical understanding of these tasks is sorely lacking, and also because the low correlations mean that it's hard to discern the pattern of correlations – when the highest correlations is 0.4, one needs very narrow confidence intervals to be confident of the ordering of the tasks.

Treviño et al. (2021) reported data from a web-based test of an opportunity sample of more than 400 participants aged 18 to 89. The test included cognitive, attentional, and common neuropsychological tasks: arithmetic word problems, the trail-making task, digit span, digit symbol coding, letter cancellation, spatial span, approximate number sense, flanker interference, gradual onset continuous performance, spatial configuration visual search, and visual working memory as well as MOT. MOT had among the highest reliabilities, at 0.92. MOT performance had little correlation with performance on the task designed to measure sustained attention over an extended period – about five minutes, using the gradual-onset continual performance task (Fortenbaugh et al., 2015). This supports the tentative conclusion that the ability to sustain attention without lapses is not an important determinant of tracking performance.

In the Treviño et al. (2021) inventory, the task that most resembled the counting task found by Huang et al. (2012) to have a high correlation with MOT was an approximate number sense task, which had a moderate correlation of 0.3. The approximate number sense task differed from the counting task of Huang et al. (2012) by not testing the subitizing (less than five items) range, which might help explain the apparent discrepancy. Indeed, Eayrs and Lavie (2018) found, using hierarchical regression, that subitizing made a contribution to predicting MOT performance that was somewhat separate to that of an estimation task using larger set sizes.

The tasks with the highest correlations with MOT in the data of Treviño et al. (2021) were visual working memory, spatial span, letter cancellation, and digit symbol coding, all at around 0.5. As the authors pointed out, the letter cancellation and digit symbol coding tasks are complex tasks believed to reflect a number of abilities. This makes it hard to interpret their correlation with MOT. Spatial span and visual working memory are quite different from MOT, but similar to each other in that they both involve short-term memory for multiple visual stimuli.

Overall, there is a reasonable level of agreement across these individual-differences studies, as well as others not reviewed here, such as Trick et al. (2012). Visual working memory has a robust correlation with MOT performance, which is interesting because superficially, MOT imposes little to no memory demand. Many researchers conceive of tracking as simply the simultaneous allocation of multifocal attention to multiple objects, with a process autonomous to memory causing the foci of attention to move along with the moving targets.

From the consistently strong correlation of MOT performance with visual working memory, it is tempting to conclude that mechanistically the two tasks are tightly linked. However, it must be remembered that working memory tasks are among the best predictors of a wide range of tasks, including intelligence as well as the Stroop task, spatial cuing, and task switching (e.g. Redick and Engle, 2006).

11.2 Going Deeper

Variation in multiple object tracking is unlikely to be caused by variation in just one ability. We now understand that tracking performance can be limited by spatial interference and temporal interference, as well as less task-specific factors such as lapses of attention.

Unfortunately, no individual difference study to date seems to have used task variations to partial out components of MOT and determine whether they show different patterns of correlations with other tasks. With other tasks, using static stimuli, studies have revealed substantial individual differences in spatial interference (Petrov and Meleshkevich, 2011), such as larger crowding zones in some types of dyslexia (Joo et al., 2018). It's possible that these differences are responsible for a large part of the inter-individual differences in MOT. There is also evidence that training with action video games can reduce spatial interference and improve reading ability (Bertoni et al., 2019), which makes it especially important that spatial interference be investigated further.

With the growth of online testing, the sample sizes required for individual difference studies have become easier to obtain, and so individual differences are a promising future direction. However, researchers should be aware of the issues that are important for individual-differences studies, such as the pitfalls described in the beginning of this section.

12 Towards the Real World

The change detection literature is an inspiring example of how lessons from a task can inform real-world practice. Without knowledge of change detection results, some practitioners, such as coaches of team sports, likely subscribed to the naive view of visual perception and attention that we are simultaneously aware of the identities of all the objects in a scene, such that unless a player actually disappears or hides behind something or someone, players should know where everyone in front of us on the basketball court, or the soccer field, is at all times (Scholl et al., 2004). Similarly, during driving many people seem to assume that they are aware of all hazards in their visual field.

While change blindness demonstrations have dispelled naive beliefs about visual awareness of change, still people assume that if they are actively attending to a moving object, they will be aware of its features. As we have seen (Section 10), this is not true. Tracking does facilitate change detection however, as found in a driving simulator study by Lochner and Trick (2014).

Very few empirical studies have established strong links between real-world situations and laboratory MOT tasks or its underlying abilities. Bowers et al.

(2013) found that laboratory MOT performance did not predict driving test performance as well as the Montreal Cognitive Assessment task, a trail-making task, or a useful field-of-view task. The aforementioned driving simulator study by Lochner and Trick (2014) found that drivers were more accurate at localizing which of multiple lead vehicles braked if it was a tracking target, but there was no advantage in terms of braking response time.

Mackenzie et al. (2021) used a multiple object avoidance (MOA) task where the user, in a task reminiscent of Asteroids (Section 1), controlled one of the balls with a mouse, trying to prevent it from colliding with the other balls. Strong correlations were found with years of driving experience and driving simulator performance. Some of the same authors also found that MOA performance correlated better with driving performance than conventional MOT (Mackenzie and Harris, 2017). This may be because MOA includes motor control, which is necessary for driving, but is not required for MOT.

Some teams of researchers have repeatedly found evidence that MOT performance predicts in-game performance in soccer and other sports, and have also reported evidence that training on MOT tasks can enhance skill in sports. Unfortunately, the evidence is not strong (Vater et al., 2021). Given the poor record of computer-based training tasks (sometimes called "brain training") in improving skills in other real-world domains (Simons et al., 2016), we should be skeptical that MOT training has benefits until rigorous evidence is provided.

13 Progress and Recommendations

Near the beginning of this Element, I suggested that five findings about multiple object tracking were particularly important. Now that I've explained them and gone through the associated evidence, it's time to sum up. The five findings are:

(1) The number of moving objects humans can track is limited, but not to a particular number such as four or five (Section 3).

(2) The number of targets has little effect on spatial interference, whereas it greatly increases temporal interference (Section 5).

(3) Predictability of movement paths benefits tracking only for one or two targets, not for more (Section 6).

(4) Tracking capacity is hemifield-specific: capacity nearly doubles when targets are presented in different hemifields (Section 9).

(5) When tracking multiple targets, people often don't know which target is which, and updating of non-location features is poor (Section 10).

The first theory of multiple object tracking, Pylyshyn's FINST theory, debuted in the first paper that established that people can actually do the task.

Although hundreds of MOT experiments have been published since then, as of this writing, the FINST theory is the only theory mentioned on the Wikipedia page for MOT (Editors, 2021). Based on what they write in their papers, many active researchers as well as Wikipedia's editors do not seem to appreciate how much the main points of FINST theory have been rebutted. Core to the theory was the idea that tracking is mediated by a small set of discrete and pre-attentive indices. As we have seen, however, as object speed increases, the number of targets that can be tracked steadily decreases, to just one target, which doesn't sit well with a fixed set of indices (Alvarez and Franconeri, 2007; Holcombe and Chen, 2012; see also Scholl, 2008). Instead, it suggests that tracking reflects a more continuous resource that can both be allocated entirely to one or two objects and spread thinly among several objects. However, it could also be explained by a process that has to serially switch among the targets.

Another prediction of FINST theory was that participants would be aware of which target is which among the targets they are tracking. Pylyshyn himself reported evidence against this, to his credit, and the evidence that updating of target identities is poor has increased since then (important finding #5 above). Explaining the dissociation between position updating and non-position maintenance and updating of features is an integral part of two recent theories, by Li et al. (2019) and by Lovett et al. (2019). Both concur with FINST theory that position updating happens in parallel, but they suggest that other features of targets are maintained and updated by a process that switches among the targets one-by-one.

Humans' poor awareness of which monitored object is which has consequences for the quest to explain our cognitive abilities. Our minds can represent structure in a content-independent fashion, such as with language, where syntax involves structure with distinct roles, e.g. using the word "giving" can involve a giver, a recipient, and item. A recent paper suggested that this could be implemented by Pylyshyn's FINSTs (O'Reilly et al., 2022). As we have seen, however, during multiple object tracking the distinct identities of the targets often are not represented, so this approach to explaining cognition may not work.

In positing a serial process for updating of features other than position, Lovett et al. (2019) further proposed that the serial process can compute the motion history of a target. This can explain important finding #3, that predictability of motion trajectories yields a measurable advantage only when there are only a few targets (Howe and Holcombe, 2012; Luu and Howe, 2015), because with more targets, the benefit may be too small to be detectable.

In summary, spatial selection appears to occur in parallel, at a hemifield-specific processing stage, with other features subsequently updated and linked in at a visual field-wide, possibly serial, process. Some evidence about position updating, however, suggests that it may be more limited-capacity than it appears, which I grapple with in another manuscript (Holcombe, 2022).

13.1 Recommendations for Future Work

The MOT paradigm is important not only because of the insights that its findings provide, but also because it has the potential to reveal many more insights about human abilities. MOT's high test-retest reliability, on the order of .8 or .9, has been found to be the higher than other attentional tasks. High reliability means that MOT results are often highly credible (because with a non-noisy task, less data is needed to have high statistical power) and have high potential for revealing individual differences (Section 11).

The discovery that tracking's capacity limit reflects two resources, one in each hemisphere, was one of the greatest advances in tracking research, but it's disappointing how little that discovery has been built upon. Consider, for example, the issue of whether tracking draws on the same mental resources as other tasks. FINST theory proposed that the tracking process is preattentive, but dual-task studies show substantial interference from other tasks (Oksama and Hyönä, 2016; Alnaes et al., 2014). Sadly, however, such studies do not seem to have ruled out the possibility that these findings were caused entirely by a process with a capacity of only one object (what I have called System B) rather than the hemifield-specific tracking processes. "Carving nature at its joints," or dissociating the components of a biological system, is important for scientific progress but can be difficult in psychology (Fodor, 1983) – general cognition (System B) can do many different things and thereby contaminate the study of any processing specific to object tracking. Testing for hemifield specificity can help us tease System B apart.

I'd like to see fewer missed opportunities to study what makes tracking distinctive, hence my top recommendations for future research emphasize this point. Those recommendations are:

- To dilute the influence of capacity-one System B processing, use several targets, not just two or three. But remember that even with several targets, a small effect could be explained by a capacity-one process. Test for hemifield specificity as that can help rule out a capacity-one process.
- Always test for hemifield specificity! In addition to it helping to rule out a factor having its effect only on a capacity-one process, we know very little about what limited-capacity brain processes are hemisphere-specific, so any results here are likely to be interesting.

- As we have seen, MOT is a complex task, so it's difficult to interpret individual differences and predict whether they will translate to other tasks. Individual-difference studies should use task variations that help isolate the component processes that contribute to overall success or failure, such as spatial interference, temporal interference, and cognitive processing.
- For computational modeling as well, don't restrict oneself to standard MOT tasks with unconstrained trajectories, as that sort of data may not constrain models very much. Show that a model succeeds at task variations that isolate component processes.

13.2 Omissions

Several topics that I originally planned to cover could not be included here due to limited space. Some of the most important are the role of retinotopic, spatiotopic, and configural representations in tracking (see [Bill et al., 2020; Howe et al., 2010b; Liu et al., 2005; Maechler et al., 2021; Meyerhoff et al., 2015; Yantis, 1992]), the role of distractor suppression, the role of surface features (Papenmeier et al., 2014), and the findings from dual-task paradigms. I hope those readers whose favorite topic was left out can take some consolation in the fact that my own favorite, the temporal limits on tracking (Holcombe and Chen, 2013; Roudaia and Faubert, 2017), also was not covered. Because that topic has major implications for what the tracking resource actually does during tracking, and whether processing is serial or parallel, I have a separate manuscript about it (Holcombe, 2022).

References

Aczel, B., Palfi, B., Szollosi, A. et al. (2018). Quantifying support for the null hypothesis in psychology: An empirical investigation. *Advances in Methods and Practices in Psychological Science*, 1(3):357–366.

Agosta, S., Magnago, D., Tyler, S. et al. (2017). The pivotal role of the right parietal lobe in temporal attention. *Journal of Cognitive Neuroscience*, 29(5):805–815.

Alnaes, D., Sneve, M. H., Espeseth, T., Pieter, S. H., and Laeng, B. (2014). Pupil size signals mental effort deployed during multiple object tracking and predicts brain activity in the dorsal attention network and the locus coeruleus. *Journal of Vision*, 14:1–20.

Alvarez, G. and Scholl, B. J. (2005). How does attention select and track spatially extended objects? New effects of attentional concentration and amplification. *Journal of Experimental Psychology: General*, 134(4):461–476.

Alvarez, G. A. and Cavanagh, P. (2005). Independent resources for attentional tracking in the left and right visual hemifields. *Psychological Science*, 16(8):637–643.

Alvarez, G. A. and Franconeri, S. L. (2007). How many objects can you track? Evidence for a resource-limited attentive tracking mechanism. *Journal of Vision*, 7(13):14,1–10.

Alvarez, G. A., Gill, J., and Cavanagh, P. (2012). Anatomical constraints on attention: Hemifield independence is a signature of multifocal spatial selection. *Journal of Vision*, 12(5)9, 1–20.

Alvarez, G. A. and Oliva, A. (2009). Spatial ensemble statistics are efficient codes that can be represented with reduced attention. *Proceedings of the National Academy of Sciences of the United States of America*, 106(18):7345–7350.

Alzahabi, R. and Cain, M. S. (2021). Ensemble perception during multiple-object tracking. *Attention, Perception, & Psychophysics*, 83(3):1263–1274.

Anstis, S. (1990). Imperceptible intersections: The chopstick illusion. In A. Blake and T. Troscianko, editors, *AI and the Eye*, 105–117. John Wiley, London.

Awh, E. and Pashler, H. (2000). Evidence for split attentional foci. *Journal of Experimental Psychology: Human Perception and Performance*, 26(2):834–846.

Battelli, L., Alvarez, G., Carlson, T., and Pascual-Leone, A. (2009). The role of the parietal lobe in visual extinction studied with transcranial magnetic stimulation. *Journal of Cognitive Neuroscience*, 21(10):1946–1955.

Battelli, L., Cavanagh, P., Intriligator, J., Tramo, M. J., and Barton, J. J. S. (2001). Unilateral right parietal damage leads to bilateral deficit for high-level motion. *Neuron*, 32(1992):985–995.

Battelli, L., Cavanagh, P., Martini, P., and Barton, J. J. S. (2003). Bilateral deficits of transient visual attention in right parietal patients. *Brain: A Journal of Neurology*, 126(Pt 10):2164–2174.

Bertoni, S., Franceschini, S., Ronconi, L., Gori, S., and Facoetti, A. (2019). Is excessive visual crowding causally linked to developmental dyslexia? *Neuropsychologia*, 130:107–117.

Bettencourt, K. C., Michalka, S. W., and Somers, D. C. (2011). Shared filtering processes link attentional and visual short-term memory capacity limits. *Journal of Vision*, 11(10):22–22.

Bex, P. J., Dakin, S. C., and Simmers, A. J. (2003). The shape and size of crowding for moving targets. *Vision Research*, 43(27):2895–2904.

Bill, J., Pailian, H., Gershman, S. J., and Drugowitsch, J. (2020). Hierarchical structure is employed by humans during visual motion perception. *Proceedings of the National Academy of Sciences*, 117(39): 24581–24589.

Bouma, H. (1970). Interaction effects in parafoveal letter recognition. *Nature*, 226(5241):177–178.

Bowers, A. R., Anastasio, R. J., Sheldon, S. S. et al. (2013). Can we improve clinical prediction of at-risk older drivers? *Accident Analysis & Prevention*, 59: 537–547.

Burt, P. and Sperling, G. (1981). Time, distance, and feature trade-offs in visual apparent motion. *Psychological Review*, 88(2):171.

Button, K. S., Ioannidis, J. P., Mokrysz, C. et al. (2013). Power failure: Why small sample size undermines the reliability of neuroscience. *Nature Reviews Neuroscience*, 14(May): 365–376.

Callahan-Flintoft, C., Holcombe, A. O., and Wyble, B. (2020). A delay in sampling information from temporally autocorrelated visual stimuli. *Nature Communications*, 11(1):1852.

Carlson, T., Alvarez, G., and Cavanagh, P. (2007). Quadrantic deficit reveals anatomical constraints on selection. *Proceedings of the National Academy of Sciences of the United States of America*, 104(33):13496–13500.

Chen, W.-Y., Howe, P. D., and Holcombe, A. O. (2013). Resource demands of object tracking and differential allocation of the resource. *Attention, Perception & Psychophysics*, 75(4):710–725.

Chesney, D. L. and Haladjian, H. H. (2011). Evidence for a shared mechanism used in multiple-object tracking and subitizing. *Attention, Perception, & Psychophysics*, 73(8):2457–2480.

Chin, J. M., Pickett, J. T., Vazire, S., and Holcombe, A. O. (2021). Questionable research practices and open science in quantitative criminology. *Journal of Quantitative Criminology*. https://doi.org/10.1007/s10940-021-09525-6.

Cohen, M., Pinto, Y., Howe, P. D. L., and Horowitz, T. S. (2011). The what-where trade-off in multiple-identity tracking. *Attention, Perception & Psychophysics*, 73(5):1422–1434.

Cohen, M. R. and Maunsell, J. H. (2011). Using neuronal populations to study the mechanisms underlying spatial and feature attention. *Neuron*, 70(6):1192–1204.

Cotton, P. L. and Smith, A. T. (2007). Contralateral visual hemifield representations in the human pulvinar nucleus. *Journal of Neurophysiology*, 98(3):1600–1609.

Cowan, N. (2001). The magical number 4 in short-term memory: A reconsideration of mental storage capacity. *Behavioral and Brain Sciences*, 24(1):87–114.

Crowe, E. M., Howard, C. J., Attwood, A. S., and Kent, C. (2019). Goal-directed unequal attention allocation during multiple object tracking. *Attention, Perception, & Psychophysics*, 81(5):1312–1326.

Culham, J. C., Cavanagh, P., and Kanwisher, N. G. (2001). Attention response functions: Characterizing brain areas using fMRI activation during parametric variations of attentional load. *Neuron*, 32(4):737–745.

Davis, G. and Holmes, A. (2005). Reversal of object-based benefits in visual attention. *Visual Cognition*, 12(5):817–846.

Delvenne, J. (2012). Visual short-term memory and the bilateral field advantage. In Kalivas, G and Petralia, SF, editors, *Short-Term Memory: New Research*. Nova.

Delvenne, J.-F. (2005). The capacity of visual short-term memory within and between hemifields. *Cognition*, 96(3):B79–B88.

Dimond, S. and Beaumont, G. (1971). Use of two cerebral hemispheres to increase brain capacity. *Nature*, 232(5308):270–271.

Doran, M. M. and Hoffman, J. E. (2010). The role of visual attention in multiple object tracking: Evidence from ERPs. *Attention, Perception, & Psychophysics*, 72(1):33–52.

Drew, T., Mance, I., Horowitz, T. S., Wolfe, J. M., and Vogel, E. K. (2014). A soft handoff of attention between cerebral hemispheres. *Current Biology*, 24(10):1133–1137.

Eayrs, J. and Lavie, N. (2018). Establishing individual differences in perceptual capacity. *Journal of Experimental Psychology: Human Perception and Performance*, 44(8):1240.

Editors, W. (2021). Multiple object tracking. *Wikipedia*. https://en.wikipedia .org/wiki/Multiple_object_tracking.

Edwards, G., Berestova, A., and Battelli, L. (2021). Behavioral gain following isolation of attention. *Scientific Reports*, 11(1):19329.

Egly, R., Driver, J., and Rafal, R. D. (1994). Shifting visual attention between objects and locations: Evidence from normal and parietal lesion subjects. *Journal of Experimental Psychology: General*, 123(2):161.

Falkner, A. L., Krishna, B. S., and Goldberg, M. E. (2010). Surround suppression sharpens the priority map in the lateral intraparietal area. *The Journal of Neuroscience: The Official Journal of the Society for Neuroscience*, 30(38):12787–12797.

Faubert, J. and Von Grunau, M. (1995). The influence of two spatially distinct primers and attribute priming on motion induction. *Vision Research*, 35(22):3119–3130.

Fecteau, J. and Munoz, D. (2006). Salience, relevance, and firing: A priority map for target selection. *Trends in Cognitive Sciences*, 10(8):382–390.

Fehd, H. M. and Seiffert, A. E. (2008). Eye movements during multiple object tracking: Where do participants look? *Cognition*, 108(1):201–209.

Fencsik, D. E., Klieger, S. B., and Horowitz, T. S. (2007). The role of location and motion information in the tracking and recovery of moving objects. *Perception & Psychophysics*, 69(4):567–577.

Feria, C. S. (2013). Speed has an effect on multiple-object tracking independently of the number of close encounters between targets and distractors. *Attention, Perception & Psychophysics*, 75(1):53–67.

Fodor, J. A. (1983). *The Modularity of Mind*. MIT Press, Cambridge, MA.

Fortenbaugh, F. C., DeGutis, J., Germine, L. et al. (2015). Sustained attention across the life span in a sample of 10,000: Dissociating ability and strategy. *Psychological Science*, 26(9):1497–1510.

Fougnie, D. and Marois, R. (2006). Distinct capacity limits for attention and working memory: Evidence from attentive tracking and visual working memory paradigms. *Psychological Science*, 17(6):526–534.

Francis, G. and Thunell, E. (2022). Excess success in articles on object-based attention. *Attention, Perception & Psychophysics*, 84: 700–714.

Franconeri, S. L. (2013). The nature and status of visual resources. In Reisberg, D., editor, *Oxford Handbook of Cognitive Psychology*, volume 8481. Oxford University Press, Oxford.

Franconeri, S. L., Alvarez, G. A., and Cavanagh, P. (2013a). Flexible cognitive resources : Competitive content maps for attention and memory. *Trends in Cognitive Sciences*, 17(3):134–141.

Franconeri, S. L., Alvarez, G. A., and Cavanagh, P. (2013b). Resource theory is not a theory: A reply to Holcombe. Online comment on Trends in Cognitive Sciences, 17(3): 134–141.

Franconeri, S. L., Jonathan, S. V., and Scimeca, J. M. (2010). Tracking multiple objects is limited only by object spacing, not by speed, time, or capacity. *Psychological Science*, 21(7):920–925.

Franconeri, S. L., Lin, J. Y., Pylyshyn, Z. W., Fisher, B., and Enns, J. T. (2008). Evidence against a speed limit in multiple-object tracking. *Psychonomic Bulletin & Review*, 15(4):802–808.

Goodale, M. A. and Milner, A. (1992). Separate visual pathways for perception and action. *Trends in Neurosciences*, 15(1):20–25.

Gurnsey, R., Roddy, G., and Chanab, W. (2011). Crowding is size and eccentricity dependent. *Journal of Vision*, 11:1–17.

Hagler Jr, D. J. and Sereno, M. I. (2006). Spatial maps in frontal and prefrontal cortex. *Neuroimage*, 29(2):567–577.

Harrison, W. J., Ayeni, A. J., and Bex, P. J. (2019). Attentional selection and illusory surface appearance. *Scientific Reports*, 9(1):2227.

Harrison, W. J. and Rideaux, R. (2019). Voluntary control of illusory contour formation. *Attention, Perception, & Psychophysics*, 81(5):1522–1531.

Hayhoe, M. M., Bensinger, D. G., and Ballard, D. H. (1998). Task constraints in visual working memory. *Vision Research*, 38(1):125–137.

Hedge, C., Powell, G., and Sumner, P. (2018). The reliability paradox: Why robust cognitive tasks do not produce reliable individual differences. *Behavior Research Methods*, 50(3):1166–1186.

Hemond, C. C., Kanwisher, N. G., and Op de Beeck, H. P. (2007). A preference for contralateral stimuli in human object- and face-selective cortex. *PLoS ONE*, 2(6):e574.

Hogendoorn, H., Carlson, T. A., and Verstraten, F. A. (2007). The time course of attentive tracking. *Journal of Vision*, 7(14):2, 1–10.

Holcombe, A. O. (2009). Temporal binding favours the early phase of colour changes, but not of motion changes, yielding the colour-motion asynchrony illusion. *Visual Cognition*, 17(1–2):232–253.

Holcombe, A. O. (2019). Comment: Capacity limits are caused by a finite resource, not spatial competition, 1–2. https://psyarxiv.com/2tg4n/. DOI: 10.31234/osf.io/2tg4n.

Holcombe, A. O. Temporal crowding imposes strong constraints on multiple object tracking. Unpublished manuscript. http://trackinglimits.whatanimalssee.com/

Holcombe, A. O., Chen, W., and Howe, P. D. L. (2014). Object tracking: Absence of long-range spatial interference supports resource theories. *Journal of Vision*, 14(6):1–21.

Holcombe, A. O. and Chen, W.-Y. (2012). Exhausting attentional tracking resources with a single fast-moving object. *Cognition*, 123(2).

Holcombe, A. O. and Chen, W.-y. (2013). Splitting attention reduces temporal resolution from 7 Hz for tracking one object to <3 Hz when tracking three. *Journal of Vision*, 13(1):1–19.

Holt, J. L. and Delvenne, J.-F. (2015). A bilateral advantage for maintaining objects in visual short term memory. *Acta Psychologica*, 154:54–61.

Horowitz, T. and Treisman, A. (1994). Attention and apparent motion. *Spatial Vision*, 8(2):193–220.

Horowitz, T. S., Klieger, S. B., Fencsik, D. E., Yang, K. K., a Alvarez, G., and Wolfe, J. M. (2007). Tracking unique objects. *Perception & Psychophysics*, 69(2):172–184.

Howard, C. J. and Holcombe, A. O. (2008). Tracking the changing features of multiple objects: Progressively poorer perceptual precision and progressively greater perceptual lag. *Vision Research*, 48(9):1164–1180.

Howard, C. J., Masom, D., and Holcombe, A. O. (2011). Position representations lag behind targets in multiple object tracking. *Vision Research*, 51(17): 1907-1919. https://doi.org/10.1016/j.visres.2011.07.001.

Howe, P. D. and Holcombe, A. O. (2012). Motion information is sometimes used as an aid to the visual tracking of objects. *Journal of Vision*, 12(13):1–10.

Howe, P. D., Horowitz, T. S., Wolfe, J., and Livingstone, M. S. (2009). Using fMRI to distinguish components of the multiple object tracking task. *Journal of Vision*, 9(4):1–11.

Howe, P. D., Incledon, N. C., and Little, D. R. (2012). Can attention be confined to just part of a moving object? Revisiting target-distractor merging in multiple object tracking. *PloS One*, 7(7):e41491.

Howe, P. D. L., Cohen, M. A., and Horowitz, T. S. (2010a). Distinguishing between parallel and serial accounts of multiple object tracking. *Journal of Vision*, 10:1–13.

Howe, P. D. L. and Ferguson, A. (2015). The identity-location binding problem. *Cognitive Science*, 39(7):1622–1645.

Howe, P. D. L., Holcombe, A. O., Lapierre, M. D., and Cropper, S. J. (2013). Visually tracking and localizing expanding and contracting objects. *Perception*, 42(12):1281–1300.

Howe, P. D. L., Pinto, Y., and Horowitz, T. S. (2010b). The coordinate systems used in visual tracking. *Vision Research*, 50(23):2375–2380.

Huang, L., Mo, L., and Li, Y. (2012). Measuring the interrelations among multiple paradigms of visual attention: An individual differences approach. *Journal of Experimental Psychology: Human Perception and Performance*, 38(2):414.

Hudson, C., Howe, P. D., and Little, D. R. (2012). Hemifield effects in multiple identity tracking. *PloS One*, 7(8):e43796.

Hung, G. K., Wilder, J., Curry, R., and Julesz, B. (1995). Simultaneous better than sequential for brief presentations. *Journal of the Optical Society of America. A, Optics, Image Science, and Vision*, 12(3):441–449.

Hyönä, J., Li, J., and Oksama, L. (2019). Eye behavior during multiple object tracking and multiple identity tracking. *Vision*, 3(3):37.

Intriligator, J. and Cavanagh, P. (2001). The spatial resolution of visual attention. *Cognitive Psychology*, 43(3):171–216.

James, W. (1890). *The Principles of Psychology, Vol I.* Henry Holt, New York, US.

Johansson, G. (1973). Visual perception of biological motion and a model for its analysis. *Perception & Psychophysics*, 14: 201–211.

John, L. K., Loewenstein, G., and Prelec, D. (2012). Measuring the prevalence of questionable research practices with incentives for truth telling. *Psychological Science*, 23(5):524–532.

Joo, S. J., White, A. L., Strodtman, D. J., and Yeatman, J. D. (2018). Optimizing text for an individual's visual system: The contribution of visual crowding to reading difficulties. *Cortex*, 103:291–301.

Jovicich, J., Peters, R. J., Koch, C. et al. (2001). Brain areas specific for attentional load in a motion-tracking task. *Journal of cognitive neuroscience*, 13(8):1048–58.

Kahneman, D., Treisman, A., and Gibbs, B. J. (1992). The reviewing of object files: Object-specific integration of information. *Cognitive Psychology*, 24(2):175–219.

Kennedy, G. J., Tripathy, S. P., and Barrett, B. T. (2009). Early age-related decline in the effective number of trajectories tracked in adult human vision. *Journal of Vision*, 9(2):21–21.

Kimchi, R. and Peterson, M. A. (2008). Figure-ground segmentation can occur without attention. *Psychological Science*, 19(7):660–668.

Kolers, P. A. and Pomerantz, J. R. (1971). Figural change in apparent motion. *Journal of Experimental Psychology*, 87(1):99.

Korte, W. (1923). über die Gestaltauffassung im indirekten Sehen. *Zeitschrift für Psychologie*, 93:17–82.

Kubovy, M., Holcombe, A. O., and Wagemans, J. (1998). On the lawfulness of grouping by proximity. *Cognitive Psychology*, 35(1):71–98.

Li, J., Oksama, L., and Hyönä, J. (2019). Model of Multiple Identity Tracking (MOMIT) 2.0: Resolving the serial vs. parallel controversy in tracking. *Cognition*, 182:260–274.

Liu, G., Austen, E. L., Booth, K. S. et al. (2005). Multiple-object tracking is based on scene, not retinal, coordinates. *Journal of experimental psychology. Human Perception and Performance*, 31(2):235–247.

Liu, T., Jiang, Y., Sun, X., and He, S. (2009). Reduction of the crowding effect in spatially adjacent but cortically remote visual stimuli. *Current Biology*, 19(2):127–32.

Lo, S.-Y. and Holcombe, A. O. (2014). How do we select multiple features? Transient costs for selecting two colors rather than one, persistent costs for color–location conjunctions. *Attention, Perception, & Psychophysics*, 76(2):304–321.

Lochner, M. J. and Trick, L. M. (2014). Multiple-object tracking while driving: The multiple-vehicle tracking task. *Attention, Perception & Psychophysics*, 76: 2326–2345. https://doi.org/10.3758/s13414-014-0694-3.

Lou, H., Lorist, M. M., and Pilz, K. S. (2020). Individual differences in the temporal dynamics of attentional selection. https://doi.org/10.31234/osf.io/w5b43.

Lovett, A., Bridewell, W., and Bello, P. (2019). Selection enables enhancement: An integrated model of object tracking. *Journal of Vision*, 19(14): 23.

Luck, S. J., Hillyard, S. A., Mangun, G. R., and Gazzaniga, M. S. (1989). Independent hemispheric attentional systems mediate visual search in split-brain patients. *Nature*, 342(6249):543–545.

Luck, S. J., Hillyard, S. A., Mangun, G. R., and Gazzaniga, M. S. (1994). Independent attentional scanning in the separated hemispheres of split-brain patients. *Journal of Cognitive Neuroscience*, 6(1):84–91.

Lukavský, J. (2013). Eye movements in repeated multiple object tracking. *Journal of Vision*, 13(7):1–16.

Lunghi, C., Burr, D. C., and Morrone, C. (2011). Brief periods of monocular deprivation disrupt ocular balance in human adult visual cortex. *Current Biology*, 21(14):R538–R539.

Luu, T. and Howe, P. D. L. (2015). Extrapolation occurs in multiple object tracking when eye movements are controlled. *Attention, Perception, & Psychophysics*, 77: 1919–1929. https://doi.org/10.3758/s13414-015-0891-8.

Mackenzie, A. K. and Harris, J. M. (2017). A link between attentional function, effective eye movements, and driving ability. *Journal of Experimental Psychology: Human Perception and Performance*, 43(2):381.

Mackenzie, A. K., Vernon, M. L., Cox, P. R. et al. (2021). The Multiple Object Avoidance (MOA) task measures attention for action: Evidence from driving and sport. *Behavior Research Methods*, 54: 1508–1529.

Maechler, M. R., Cavanagh, P., and Tse, P. U. (2021). Attentional tracking takes place over perceived rather than veridical positions. *Attention, Perception, & Psychophysics*, 83: 1455–1462.

Makovski, T. and Jiang, Y. V. (2009). Feature binding in attentive tracking of distinct objects. *Visual Cognition*, 17(1–2):180–194.

Mareschal, I., Morgan, M. J., and Solomon, J. A. (2010). Attentional modulation of crowding. *Vision Research*, 50(8):805–809.

Maruya, K., Holcombe, A. O., and Nishida, S. (2013). Rapid encoding of relationships between spatially remote motion signals. *Journal of Vision*, 13(4):1–20.

Matthews, N. and Welch, L. (2015). Left visual field attentional advantage in judging simultaneity and temporal order. *Journal of Vision*, 15(2):7.

Merkel, C., Hopf, J.-M., and Schoenfeld, M. A. (2017). Spatio-temporal dynamics of attentional selection stages during multiple object tracking. *NeuroImage*, 146:484–491.

Merkel, C., Stoppel, C. M., Hillyard, S. A. et al. (2014). Spatio-temporal patterns of brain activity distinguish strategies of multiple-object tracking. *Journal of Cognitive Neuroscience*, 26(1):28–40.

Mesulam, M.-M. (1999). Spatial attention and neglect: Parietal, frontal and cingulate contributions to the mental representation and attentional targeting of salient extrapersonal events. *Philosophical Transactions of the Royal Society of London. Series B: Biological Sciences*, 354(1387):1325–1346.

Meyerhoff, H. S. and Papenmeier, F. (2020). Individual differences in visual attention: A short, reliable, open-source, and multilingual test of multiple object tracking in PsychoPy. *Behavior Research Methods*, 52(6):2556–2566.

Meyerhoff, H. S., Papenmeier, F., Jahn, G., and Huff, M. (2015). Distractor locations influence multiple object tracking beyond interobject spacing: Evidence from equidistant distractor displacements. *Experimental Psychology*, 62(3):170–180.

Miller, G. A. (1956). The magical number seven, plus or minus two: Some limits on our capacity for processing information. *Psychological Review*, 63(2):81.

Minami, T., Shinkai, T., and Nakauchi, S. (2019). Hemifield crossings during multiple object tracking affect task performance and steady-state visual evoked potentials. *Neuroscience*, 409:162–168.

Nakayama, K., He, Z. J., and Shimojo, S. (1995). Visual surface representation: A critical link between lower-level and higher-level vision. *Visual Cognition: An Invitation to Cognitive Science*, 2:1–70.

Neisser, U. (1963). Decision-time without reaction-time: Experiments in visual scanning. *The American Journal of Psychology*, 76(3): 376.

Ngiam, W. X., Khaw, K. L., Holcombe, A. O., and Goodbourn, P. T. (2019). Visual working memory for letters varies with familiarity but not complexity. *Journal of Experimental Psychology: Learning, Memory, and Cognition*, 45(10):1761.

Norman, D. A. and Bobrow, D. G. (1975). On data-limited and resource-limited processes. *Cognitive Psychology*, 7:44–64.

Nummenmaa, L., Oksama, L., Glerean, E., and Hyönä, J. (2017). Cortical circuit for binding object identity and location during multiple-object tracking. *Cerebral Cortex*, 27(1):162–172.

Oberauer, K. (2002). Access to information in working memory: Exploring the focus of attention. *Journal of Experimental Psychology: Learning, Memory, and Cognition*, 28(3):411.

Oberauer, K. et al. (2018). Benchmarks for models of short-term and working memory. *Psychological Bulletin*, 144(9):885.

Oksama, L. and Hyönä, J. (2004). Is multiple object tracking carried out automatically by an early vision mechanism independent of higher-order cognition? An individual difference approach. *Visual Cognition*, 11(5):631–671.

Oksama, L. and Hyönä, J. (2016). Position tracking and identity tracking are separate systems: Evidence from eye movements. *Cognition*, 146:393–409.

Ongchoco, J. D. K. and Scholl, B. J. (2019). How to create objects with your mind: From object-based attention to attention-based objects. *Psychological Science*, 30(11):1648–1655.

O'Regan, J. K. (1992). Solving the "real" mysteries of visual perception: The world as an outside memory. *Canadian Journal of Psychology/Revue Canadienne De Psychologie*, 46(3):461.

O'Reilly, R. C., Ranganath, C., and Russin, J. L. (2022). The Structure of Systematicity in the Brain. *Current Directions in Psychological Science*, 31(2): 124–130.

Pailian, H., Carey, S. E., Halberda, J., and Pepperberg, I. M. (2020). Age and species comparisons of visual mental manipulation ability as evidence for its development and evolution. *Scientific Reports*, 10(1):1–7.

Palmer, J. (1995). Attention in visual search: Distinguishing four causes of a set-size effect. *Current Directions in Psychological Science*, 4(4):118–123.

Papenmeier, F., Meyerhoff, H. S., Jahn, G., and Huff, M. (2014). Tracking by location and features: Object correspondence across spatiotemporal discontinuities during multiple object tracking. *Journal of Experimental Psychology: Human Perception and Performance*, 40(1):159.

Pelli, D. G. and Tillman, K. A. (2008). The uncrowded window of object recognition. *Nature Neuroscience*, 11(10):1129–1135.

Peter, U. T. (2005). Voluntary attention modulates the brightness of overlapping transparent surfaces. *Vision Research*, 45(9):1095–1098.

Peterson M. A. (2014). Low-level and high-level contributions to figure-ground organization: evidence and theoretical implications. In Wagemans J, editor. *The Oxford Handbook of Perceptual Organization*. New York: Oxford University Press.

Petrov, Y. and Meleshkevich, O. (2011). Asymmetries and idiosyncratic hot spots in crowding. *Vision Research*, 51(10):1117–1123.

Piazza, M. (2010). Neurocognitive start-up tools for symbolic number representations. *Trends in Cognitive Sciences*, 14(12):542–551.

Pilz, K. S., Roggeveen, A. B., Creighton, S. E., Bennett, P. J., and Sekuler, A. B. (2012). How prevalent is object-based attention? *PLoS ONE*, 7(2):e30693.

Proffitt, D. R., Kaiser, M. K., and Whelan, S. M. (1990). Understanding wheel dynamics. *Cognitive Psychology*, 22(3):342–373.

Pylyshyn, Z. (1989). The role of location indexes in spatial perception: A sketch of the FINST spatial-index model. *Cognition*, 32(1):65–97.

Pylyshyn, Z. (2001). Visual indexes, preconceptual objects, and situated vision. *Cognition*, 80:127–158.

Pylyshyn, Z. (2004). Some puzzling findings in multiple object tracking: I. Tracking without keeping track of object identities. *Visual Cognition*, 11(7):801–822.

Pylyshyn, Z., Burkell, J., Fisher, B. et al. (1994). Multiple parallel access in visual attention. *Canadian Journal of Experimental Psychology/Revue Canadienne De Psychologie Expérimentale*, 48(2):260.

Pylyshyn, Z. W. (2006). *Seeing and Visualizing: It's Not What You Think.* Life and Mind. MIT Press, Cambridge, Mass., 1. mit press paperback ed.

Pylyshyn, Z. W. (2007). *Things and Places: How the Mind Connects with the World.* MIT Press.

Pylyshyn, Z. W. and Storm, R. W. (1988). Tracking multiple independent targets: Evidence for a parallel tracking mechanism. *Spatial Vision*, 3(3):179–197.

Rabelo, A. L. A., Farias, J. E. M., Sarmet, M. M. et al. (2020). Questionable research practices among Brazilian psychological researchers: Results from a replication study and an international comparison. *International Journal of Psychology*, 55(4):674–683.

Redick, T. S. and Engle, R. W. (2006). Working memory capacity and attention network test performance. *Applied Cognitive Psychology: The Official Journal of the Society for Applied Research in Memory and Cognition*, 20(5):713–721.

Reichle, E. D., Liversedge, S. P., Pollatsek, A., and Rayner, K. (2009). Encoding multiple words simultaneously in reading is implausible. *Trends in Cognitive Sciences*, 13(February):115–119.

Rensink, R. (2000). Visual search for change: A probe into the nature of attentional processing. *Visual Cognition*, 7(1):345–376.

Revkin, S. K., Piazza, M., Izard, V., Cohen, L., and Dehaene, S. (2008). Does subitizing reflect numerical estimation? *Psychological science*, 19(6):607–614.

Rizzolatti, G., Umiltà, C., and Berlucchi, G. (1971). Opposite superiorities of the right and left cerbral hemispheres in discriminative reaction time to physiognomical and alphabetical material. *Brain: A Journal of Neurology*, 94(3): 431–442.

Robinson, M. M., Benjamin, A. S., and Irwin, D. E. (2020). Is there a K in capacity? Assessing the structure of visual short-term memory. *Cognitive Psychology*, 121:101305.

Roudaia, E. and Faubert, J. (2017). Different effects of aging and gender on the temporal resolution in attentional tracking. *Journal of Vision*, 17(11): 1.

Saenz, M., Buracas, G. T., and Boynton, G. M. (2002). Global effects of feature-based attention in human visual cortex. *Nature Neuroscience*, 5(7):631–632.

Saiki, J. (2002). Multiple-object permanence tracking: Limitation in maintenance and transformation of perceptual objects. *Progress in Brain Research*, 140:133–148.

Saiki, J. (2019). Robust color-shape binding representations for multiple objects in visual working memory. *Journal of Experimental Psychology: General*, 148(5):905–925.

Saiki, J. and Holcombe, A. O. (2012). Blindness to a simultaneous change of all elements in a scene, unless there is a change in summary statistics. *Journal of Vision*, 12:1–11.

Schneider, K. A. and Kastner, S. (2005). Visual responses of the human superior colliculus: A high-resolution functional magnetic resonance imaging study. *Journal of Neurophysiology*, 94(4):2491–2503.

Scholl, B. (2001). Objects and attention: The state of the art. *Cognition*, 80(1/2):1–46.

Scholl, B. J. (2008). What have we learned about attention from multiple-object tracking (and vice versa)? In D. Dedrick and L. Trick, editors, *Computation, Cognition, and Pylyshyn*, pages 49–78. MIT Press.

Scholl, B. J., Pylyshyn, Z. W., and Feldman, J. (2001). What is a visual object? Evidence from target merging in multiple object tracking. *Cognition*, 80(1-2):159–177.

Scholl, B. J., Simons, D. J., and Levin, D. T. (2004). "Change blindness" blindness: An implicit measure of a metacognitive error. In D. T. Levin, editor, *Thinking and Seeing: Visual Metacognition in Adults and Children*, pages 145–164. MIT Press, Cambridge, MA.

Schönbrodt, F. D. and Perugini, M. (2013). At what sample size do correlations stabilize? *Journal of Research in Personality*, 47(5):609–612.

Sekuler, R., McLaughlin, C., and Yotsumoto, Y. (2008). Age-related changes in attentional tracking of multiple moving objects. *Perception*, 37(6):867–876.

Sereno, A. B. and Kosslyn, S. M. (1991). Discrimination within and between hemifields: A new constraint on theories of attention. *Neuropsychologia*, 29(7):659–675.

Sereno, M. I., Pitzalis, S., and Martinez, A. (2001). Mapping of contralateral space in retinotopic coordinates by a parietal cortical area in humans. *Science*, 294(5545):1350–1354.

Shiffrin, R. M. and Gardner, G. T. (1972). Visual processing capacity and attentional control. *Journal of Experimental Psychology*, 93(1):72.

Shim, W. M., a. Alvarez, G., and Jiang, Y. V. (2008). Spatial separation between targets constrains maintenance of attention on multiple objects. *Psychonomic Bulletin & Review*, 15(2):390–397.

Shim, W. M., a Alvarez, G., Vickery, T. J., and Jiang, Y. V. (2010). The number of attentional foci and their precision are dissociated in the posterior parietal cortex. *Cerebral Cortex*, 20(6):1341–1349.

Shomstein, S. and Behrmann, M. (2008). Object-based attention: Strength of object representation and attentional guidance. *Perception & Psychophysics*, 70(1):132–144.

Shomstein, S. and Yantis, S. (2002). Object-based attention: Sensory modulation or priority setting? *Perception & Psychophysics*, 64(1):41–51.

Simon, H. A. (1969). *The Sciences of the Artificial, Reissue of the Third Edition with a New Introduction by John Laird*. MIT Press Academic, Cambridge, MA, 3rd ed.

Simons, D. J., Boot, W. R., Charness, N. et al. (2016). Do "brain-training" programs work? *Psychological Science in the Public Interest*, 17(3):103–186.

Sternberg, S. (1969). The discovery of processing stages: Extensions of Donders' method. *Acta Psychologica*, 30:276–315.

Störmer, V. S., a Alvarez, G., and Cavanagh, P. (2014). Within-hemifield competition in early visual areas limits the ability to track multiple objects with attention. *The Journal of Neuroscience : The Official Journal of the Society for Neuroscience*, 34(35):11526–11533.

Strasburger, H. (2014). Dancing letters and ticks that buzz around aimlessly: On the origin of crowding. *Perception*, 43(9):963–976.

Strong, R. W. and Alvarez, G. A. (2020). Hemifield-specific control of spatial attention and working memory: Evidence from hemifield crossover costs. *Journal of Vision*, 20(8):24.

Suchow, J. W. and Alvarez, G. A. (2011). Motion Silences Awareness of Visual Change. *Current Biology*, 21(2): 140–143.

Tadin, D., Lappin, J. S., Blake, R., and Grossman, E. D. (2002). What constitutes an efficient reference frame for vision? *Nature Neuroscience*, 5(10):1010–1015.

Tombu, M. and Seiffert, A. E. (2008). Attentional costs in multiple-object tracking. *Cognition*, 108:1–25.

Tombu, M. and Seiffert, A. E. (2011). Tracking planets and moons: Mechanisms of object tracking revealed with a new paradigm. *Attention, Perception, & Psychophysics*, 73: 738–750.

Townsend, J. T. (1990). Serial vs. parallel processing: Sometimes they look like Tweedledum and Tweedledee but they can (and should) be distinguished. *Psychological Science*, 1(1):46–54.

Treisman, A. and Gelade, G. (1980). A feature integration theory of attention. *Cognitive Psychology*, 12:97–136.

Treisman, A. and Schmidt, H. (1982). Illusory conjunctions in the perception of objects. *Cognitive Psychology*, 14:107–141.

Treisman, A. M. (1964). Verbal cues, language, and meaning in selective attention. *The American Journal of Psychology*, 77(2):206.

Treviño, M., Zhu, X., Lu, Y. Y. et al. (2021). How do we measure attention? Using factor analysis to establish construct validity of neuropsychological tests. *Cognitive Research: Principles and Implications*, 6(1):51.

Trick, L. M., Mutreja, R., and Hunt, K. (2012). Spatial and visuospatial working memory tests predict performance in classic multiple-object tracking in young adults, but nonspatial measures of the executive do not. *Attention, Perception, & Psychophysics*, 74(2):300–311.

Trick, L. M., Perl, T., and Sethi, N. (2005). Age-related differences in multiple-object tracking. *The Journals of Gerontology Series B: Psychological Sciences and Social Sciences*, 60(2):P102–P105.

Tse, P., Cavanagh, P., and Nakayama, K. (1998). The role of parsing in high-level motion processing. In Watanabe, T., editor, *High-level Motion Processing: Computational, Neurobiological, and Psychophysical Perspectives*, 249–266. MIT Press.

Tsotsos, J. K., Culhane, S. M., Wai, W. et al. (1995). Modeling visual attention via selective tuning. *Artificial Intelligence*, 78:507–545.

Tsotsos, J. K., Rodríguez-Sánchez, A. J., Rothenstein, A. L., and Simine, E. (2008). The different stages of visual recognition need different attentional binding strategies. *Brain Research*, 1225(2007):119–132.

Umemoto, A., Drew, T., Ester, E. F., and Awh, E. (2010). A bilateral advantage for storage in visual working memory. *Cognition*, 117(1):69–79.

Van der Burg, E., Cass, J., and Theeuwes, J. (2019). Changes (but not differences) in motion direction fail to capture attention. *Vision Research*, 165:54–63.

VanMarle, K. and Scholl, B. J. (2003). Attentive tracking of objects versus substances. *Psychological Science*, 14(5):498–504.

Vater, C., Gray, R., and Holcombe, A. O. (2021). A critical systematic review of the Neurotracker perceptual-cognitive training tool. *Psychonomic Bulletin & Review*, 28: 1458–1483.

Vater, C., Kredel, R., and Hossner, E.-J. (2017). Disentangling vision and attention in multiple-object tracking: How crowding and collisions affect gaze anchoring and dual-task performance. *Journal of Vision*, 17(5):1–13.

Vogel, E. K., Woodman, G. F., and Luck, S. J. (2006). The time course of consolidation in visual working memory. *Journal of Experimental Psychology. Human Perception and Performance*, 32(6):1436–1451.

Wang, L., Zhang, K., He, S., and Jiang, Y. (2010). Searching for life motion signals: Visual search asymmetry in local but not global biological-motion processing. *Psychological Science*, 21(8):1083–1089.

Wang, Y. and Vul, E. (2021). The role of kinematic properties in multiple object tracking. *Journal of Vision*, 21(3):1–15.

Wannig, A., Stanisor, L., and Roelfsema, P. R. (2011). Automatic spread of attentional response modulation along Gestalt criteria in primary visual cortex. *Nature Neuroscience*, 14(10):1243–1244.

Warren, P. A. and Rushton, S. K. (2007). Perception of object trajectory: Parsing retinal motion into self and object movement components. *Journal of Vision*, 7(11):2.

Wertheimer, M. (1912). Experimentelle Studien über das Sehen von Bewegung. *Zeitschrift für Psychologie*, 61:161–165.

White, A. L. and Carrasco, M. (2011). Feature-based attention involuntarily and simultaneously improves visual performance across locations. *Journal of Vision*, 11(6):1–10.

White, A. L., Palmer, J., and Boynton, G. M. (2018). Evidence of serial processing in visual word recognition. *Psychological Science*, 29(7):1062–1071.

White, A. L., Palmer, J., Boynton, G. M., and Yeatman, J. D. (2019). Parallel spatial channels converge at a bottleneck in anterior word-selective cortex. *Proceedings of the National Academy of Sciences*, 116(20):10087–10096.

Wilbiks, J. M. P. and Beatteay, A. (2020). Individual differences in multiple object tracking, attentional cueing, and age account for variability in the capacity of audiovisual integration. *Attention, Perception, & Psychophysics*, 82: 3521–3543.

Wolfe, J. M. (2021). Guided Search 6.0: An updated model of visual search. *Psychonomic Bulletin & Review*, 28(4):1060–1092.

Wolfe, J. M. and Bennett, S. C. (1997). Preattentive object files: Shapeless bundles of basic features. *Vision Research*, 37(1):25–43.

Wolford, G. (1975). Perturbation model for letter identification. *Psychological Review*, 82(3):184.

Wu, C.-C. and Wolfe, J. M. (2018). Comparing eye movements during position tracking and identity tracking: No evidence for separate systems. *Attention, Perception, & Psychophysics*, 80(2):453–460.

Wuerger, S., Shapley, R., and Rubin, N. (1996). "On the visually perceived direction of motion" by Hans Wallach: 60 years later. *Perception*, 25:1317–1367.

Xu, Y. and Franconeri, S. L. (2015). Capacity for Visual Features in Mental Rotation. *Psychological Science*, 26(8):1241–1251.

Yantis, S. (1992). Multielement visual tracking: Attention and perceptual organization. *Cognitive Psychology*, 24(3):295–340.

Yilmaz, A., Javed, O., and Shah, M. (2006). Object tracking: A survey. *ACM Computing Surveys*, 38(4):13.

Zelinsky, G. J. and Neider, M. B. (2008). An eye movement analysis of multiple object tracking in a realistic environment. *Visual Cognition*, 16(5):553–566.

Zelinsky, G. J. and Todor, A. (2010). The role of "rescue saccades" in tracking objects through occlusions. *Journal of Vision*, 10(14):1–13.

Zhang, J. and Mueller, S. T. (2005). A note on ROC analysis and non-parametric estimate of sensitivity. *Psychometrika*, 70(1):203–212.

Zylberberg, A., Fernández Slezak, D., Roelfsema, P. R., Dehaene, S., and Sigman, M. (2010). The brain's router: A cortical network model of serial processing in the primate brain. *PLoS Computational Biology*, 6(4):e1000765.

Cambridge Elements ☰

Perception

James T. Enns
The University of British Columbia

Editor James T. Enns is Professor at the University of British Columbia, where he researches the interaction of perception, attention, emotion, and social factors. He has previously been Editor of the *Journal of Experimental Psychology: Human Perception and Performance* and an Associate Editor at *Psychological Science, Consciousness and Cognition, Attention Perception & Psychophysics*, and *Visual Cognition*.

About the Series

The modern study of human perception includes event perception, bidirectional influences between perception and action, music, language, the integration of the senses, human action observation, and the important roles of emotion, motivation, and social factors. Each Element in the series combines authoritative literature reviews of foundational topics with forward-looking presentations of the recent developments on a given topic.

Cambridge Elements ⁼

Perception

Printed in the United States
by Baker & Taylor Publisher Services